# ESPIONAGE and COUNTER-ESPIONAGE
# HANDBOOK

## Mikhail Kryzhanovsky

PublishAmerica
Baltimore

Hardcover 9781462661602
PUBLISHED BY PUBLISHAMERICA, LLLP
www.publishamerica.com
Baltimore

Printed in the United States of America

# Contents

# About the author

**30 years of espionage experience**
Born 1958, Kolomiya, Ukraine.
Chernovtsy State University (languages, military school)
KGB Counterintelligence School (counter-espionage, crime investigation, forensic science)
KGB Intelligence Institute (espionage)
a former KGB counter-espionage secret source "Konstantin"
a former KGB counter-espionage officer
a former KGB intelligence officer
a former KGB "Nabat" anti-terror group sniper
a former SBU (Ukrainian Security Service) illegal intelligence officer
a former CIA/FBI/US Secret Service "Filament"

.

# Part 1. ESPIONAGE

**Espionage** is stealing classified or confidential information of any level. It is usually part of an institutional effort by a government or corporation.

## Components of espionage

1. *Biographic espionage* is the study of politicians, military, scientists and other persons of actual or potential importance through knowledge of their personalities and backgrounds, including educational and occupational history, individual accomplishments, idiosyncrasies and habits, position and power to make decisions.

2. *Economic espionage* is the study of the economic strengths and weaknesses of a country, including source of economic capability (any means a country has to sustain its economy), manufacturing (manufacturing processes, facilities, logistics), vulnerabilities (the degree to which a country's military would be hampered by the loss of materials or facilities), economic warfare (information on the diplomatic, financial and special steps a country may take to induce neutral countries to cease trading with its enemies).

3. *Sociological espionage* deals with people, customs, behaviors and institutions, including population (rates of increase, decrease or migrations), social characteristics (customs, values and beliefs), manpower (divisions and distribution within the workforce), health, education, welfare and public information (information services within the country).

4 *Transportation and telecommunications espionage* studies the role of transportation and telecommunications systems during military emergencies and during peacetime, including strategic railways, highways, airports, seaports, network of navigatable rivers and canals, main phone and Internet services providers.

5 *Military geographic espionage* is the study of all geographic

factors, including terrain, climate, natural resources, boundaries and population distribution.

6. *Armed forces espionage* is the integrated study of the land, sea and air forces, including strategy (military alternatives in terms of position, terrain, economics, politics ), tactics ( military deployments and operations doctrine), location, organizations, procurement, storage, distribution, weapons and training of the armed forces.

7. *Political espionage valuates* all political aspects which may affect military operations, including government structure, national policies, political dynamics (government views and reaction to events), propaganda (information and disinformation programs), special services, subversion (subversive acts sponsored by the government).

8. *Scientific and technical espionage* is the study of the country's potential and capability to support objectives through development of weapons and weapons systems, missile and space programs, nuclear energy and weapons technology, basic applied sciences.

### *Espionage collection techniques:*

1.Human intelligence
Sources :
- advisors or foreign internal defense personnel working with host nation forces or populations
- diplomatic reporting by accredited diplomats (e.g., military attachés);
- espionage clandestine reporting, defectors, access agents
- military attachés
- non-governmental organizations
- prisoners of war or detainees
- refugees;
- routine patrolling (military police, patrols, etc.)
- special reconnaissance
- traveler debriefing
2. Signals intelligence

3. Imagery intelligence
4. Measurement and signature intelligence
5. Technical Intelligence
6. Open source intelligence

**The intelligence cycle :**
a) intelligence priorities are set
b) raw information is collected
c) this information is analyzed
d) the processed information is disseminated

## U.S. National Security Strategy 2010 - ultimate stupidity

1. Globalization intensified the dangers we face - international terrorism..."
Wrong. International terrorism does not exist. Every group has a target of its own - mainly USA and Israel.
2. Renew our focus on Afghanistan as part of commitment to disrupt, dismantle and defeat al-Qa'ida.
Wrong. 10 years - we got nothing; there's nothing to renew.
3. We must pursue a strategy of global leadership.
Wrong. We can't do it unless Russia and China are disintegrated as multi-national states.
4. Our rejection of actions like tortures..."
Wrong. If CIA is not professional, if it has no damned secret sources what else they have to do ?
5. Key centers of influence - China, India, Russia.
Wrong. It's a self-rejection.
6. We will pursue engagement with hostile nations [Iran and North Korea] to test their intentions.
Wrong. They are a threat to us , because we are not a threat to them.
7. Peace between Israel and his neighbors...
Wrong Peace is not profitable over there.

8. We must maintain our military conventional superiority, while enhancing its capacity to defeat asymetric threats.

Wrong. Army can't fight asymetric threats like guerrilla, it's all about intelligence special ops.

9. Our intelligence and homeland security efforts must be integrated with our security policies, and those of our allies.

Wrong. France, Germany and Israel are into industrial espionage in America.

10. Nations must have incentives to behave responsibly, or be isolated when they do not.

Wrong. religious nations take punishment as a test.

11. Rebalance our military capabilities to excel at counterterrorism, counterinsurgency, stability operations.

Wrong. WE have to rebalance our political efforts and redirect Taliban to other targets (countries).

12. Analysts, agents and officers who protect us must have access to all relevant intelligence throughout the government.

Very wrong. Imagine a 'mole" with such access !


## U.S. National Intelligence Strategy

Why it does not work

1."At its core, this National Intelligence Strategy capitalizes on the extraordinary talents and patriotism of America's diverse intelligence professionals".

Wrong. War in Iraq, which is a complete intelligence failure because of non-stop everyday terror, proves that we do not have no damned "extraordinary" intelligence "talents".

2."Strategic objectives. Develop innovative ways to penetrate and analyze the most difficult targets".

Wrong. Innovative intelligence ways do not exist. You penetrate by recruiting a "mole" or through insider.

3."Explore alternative analytic views".

Wrong. True analysts have only one view, and it's the right one.

4."Developing new methodologies…"
Wrong. They do not exist.

5."Analysis must do more than just describe what is happening and why; it must identify a range of opportunities for (and likely consequences of) diplomatic, military, law enforcement, or homeland security action".
Wrong. Intelligence information has to be sent to State, Defense, Justice or Homeland Security Department – let them analyze, calculate opportunities, and take responsibility for the consequences.

6."Make attention to long-term and strategic analysis a part of every analyst's assigned responsibilities."
Wrong. Strategic analysis is a job for a very few .

7."The Intelligence Community must foster cross-agency collaboration at all-levels".
Wrong. It's a Christmas gift for "moles".

8. "Expand the reporting of information of intelligence value from…private sector stakeholders".
Wrong. It's a perfect opportunity for disinformation and our enemies will be happy to use it.

9. "Remove impediments to information sharing within the Community, and establish policies that reflect need-to-share (versus need-to-know) for all data , removing the "ownership" by agency of intelligence information".
Wrong. Who put forward this idea ? Another "mole" ? "Need –to-know" is the only more or less effective security tool Just give me the name – whose idea is that ?

12."Ensure the various Intelligence Community elements conducting counterintelligence activities act as a cohesive whole to undertake aggressive, unified counterintelligence operations".
Wrong. Another gift for the "moles".

13."Create a lessons-learned function to assess the effectiveness of the Community's activities as a "system of systems" in supporting national security goals".
Wrong. That's a science fiction.

14."The Intelligence Community must manage its resources by

examining national security priorities, both short and long term".

Wrong. All national security priorities, including war on terror, WMD proliferation and homeland security, are long term.

## List of KGB agents in USA

Louis Adamic, writer and spokesman for Yugoslav immigrants. During World War II, he advised the OSS on Balkan questions. Source for Golos-Bentley network via Louis Budenz.

Aldrich Ames, CIA officer spying for the Soviet Union beginning in 1985 as a 'walk-in' to the Soviet Embassy in Washington, D.C.

William Weisband, U.S. Army signals intelligence staffer

**The "Berg" – "Art" Group**

Alexander Koral, former engineer of the municipality of New York

Helen Koral, Berg's wife, housewife

Byron T. Darling, engineer for the Rubber Company

A. A. Yatskov

George Blake, United Kingdom SIS officer who betrayed existence of the Berlin Tunnel under the Soviet sector and who probably betrayed Popov.

Felix Bloch, U.S. State Department economic officer. Robert Hanssen warned Soviets about the investigation into his activities

Christopher John Boyce and Daulton Lee, American walk-in spy for the Soviet Union, known as the Falcon and the Snowman.

Buben groupLouis F. Budenz, former member of the Central Committee of the Communist Party USA, former editor of the newspaper Daily Worker, professor at Fordham University.

Robert Menaker, commercial traveler (traveling salesman) to a variety of trade firms

Salmond Franklin, without specific assignments, husband of "Rita."

Sylvia Caldwell, technical secretary for a Trotskyist group in New York City.

Lona Cohen, sentenced to 20 years; subject of Hugh Whitemore's drama for stage and TV Pack of Lies

Morris Cohen sentenced to 25 years; subject of Hugh Whitemore's drama for stage and TV Pack of Lies

Judith Coplon, NKGB counter-intelligence operative in the U.S. Department of Justice; two convictions overturned on technicalities

Eugene Dennis, senior member of the Communist Party USA leadership, sentenced to 5 years for advocating the overthrow of the U.S. government

Samuel Dickstein, Congressman from New York; before being recruited as a Soviet agent in 1937 he served as co-Chairman of a predecessor to the HUAC during hearings into the Business Plot against President Franklin D. Roosevelt[4]

Mark Gayn, journalist, The Washington Post; Amerasia case

Dieter Gerhardt, South African Navy Commodore who was convicted of spying for the Soviet Union; alleged that the Vela Incident was a joint Israeli-South African nuclear test after being released in 1994 and emigrating to Switzerland

Ben-Zion Goldberg (Benjamin Waife), journalist, contributor to Toronto Star, Saint Louis Dispatch, New York Post, Today, and The New Republic

Theodore Hall, physicist who supplied information from Los Alamos during World War II, a NYC walk-in, never prosecuted

Robert P. Hanssen, Federal Bureau of Investigation agent convicted of spying for the Soviet Union, betrayed tunnel under new Mt Alto Soviet Embassy in Washington DC; may have done most damage since Philby

Reino Häyhänen, Finn who worked in the US as a Soviet spy directed by Rudolf Abel, used the VIC cypher, defected to the US

Edward Lee Howard, ex-Central Intelligence Agency officer who sold info and escaped to Soviet Union in 1985

V. J. Jerome, sentenced to three years for advocating overthrow of U.S. government

Martin Kamen, Radiation Laboratory at the University of California, Berkeley, Manhattan Project

Walter Krivitsky

Giovanni Rossi Lomanitz, Berkeley Radiation Laboratory

Clayton J. Lonetree, U.S. Marine Embassy guard Sergeant suborned by female KGB agent ('Violetta Sanni') in Moscow, turned himself in to authorities in December 1986, convicted 1987

Jay Lovestone

Carl Marzani, Deputy Chief Photographic Presentation Branch Office of Strategic Services; United States Department of State

Alan Nunn May, physicist who supplied information about the British and American atomic bomb research to the Soviet Union

Kate Mitchell

MocaseBoris Morros, Hollywood producer

Jack Soble, sentenced to 7 years, brother of Robert Soblen

Myra Soble, sentenced to 5½ years

Robert Soblen, sentenced to life for spying at Sandia Lab, etc., but escaped to Israel, then committed suicide

Jane Zlatovski

Mark Zborowski

Perlo groupVictor Perlo, was the Chief of the Aviation Section of the War Production Board during World War II; head of branch in Research Section, Office of Price Administration Department of Commerce; Division of Monetary Research Department of the Treasury; and later the Brookings Institution

Harold Glasser, Director, Division of Monetary Research, United States Department of the Treasury; United Nations Relief and Rehabilitation Administration; War Production Board; Advisor on North African Affairs Committee; United States Treasury Representative to the Allied High Commission in Italy

Alger Hiss, Director of the Office of Special Political Affairs United States Department of State

Charles Kramer, Senate Subcommittee on War Mobilization; Office of Price Administration; National Labor Relations Board; Senate Subcommittee on Wartime Health and Education; Agricultural Adjustment Administration; Senate Subcommittee on Civil Liberties; Senate Labor and Public Welfare Committee; Democratic National Committee

Harry Magdoff, Statistical Division of War Production Board and Office of Emergency Management; Bureau of Research and Statistics, WTB; Tools Division, War Production Board; Bureau of Foreign and Domestic Commerce, United States Department of Commerce

George Perazich, Foreign Economic Administration; United Nations Relief and Rehabilitation Administration

Allen Rosenberg, Board of Economic Warfare; Chief of the Economic Institution Staff, Foreign Economic Administration; Senate Subcommittee on Civil Liberties; Senate Committee on Education and Labor; Railroad Retirement Board; Counsel to the Secretary of the National Labor Relations Board

Donald Wheeler, Office of Strategic Services Research and Analysis division

Redhead group

Hedwiga Gompertz, Wacek's wife, sent to the U.S. in 1938 to carry out fieldwork assignments, defected in 1948

Paul Massing, scientist at Columbia University's Institute of Social Research. Defected.

Laurence Duggan , former employee of the State Department. Suicide.

Franz Leopold Neumann, former consultant in the Department of Research and Analysis of the OSS

Rudolf Roessler chief of the very successful, and very odd, Lucy spy ring of World War II

Rosenberg ringJoel Barr, met Julius Rosenberg at City College of New York, then spied with him and Al Sarant at Army Signal Corps lab in New Jersey; escaped prosecution by fleeing to Soviet bloc in 1950. Died 2007.

Max Elitcher, longtime friend of Rosenberg and Sobell from their days at CCNY before testifying against them

Klaus Fuchs, physicist who supplied information about the British and American atomic bomb research to the Soviet Union; sentenced to 14 years in the UK.

Vivian Glassman, fiancée of Joel Barr

Harry Gold, courier sentenced to 30 years

David Greenglass, draftsman at Los Alamos in World War Two, gave atomic bomb drawings to his sister Ethel Rosenberg, and eventually the Soviets; sentenced to 15 years

Ruth Greenglass, escaped prosecution in exchange for her husband's testimony against his sister and brother-in-law, the Rosenbergs

Miriam Moskowitz, convicted of obstruction of justice for assisting Brothman. She was never convicted of being a spy for the Soviet Union.[6]

William Perl, active in Young Communist League at CCNY, then met Al Sarant at Columbia University; served 5 years for perjury

Morton Sobell, involved with Barr, Perl and Julius Rosenberg at CCNY; sentenced to 30 years at Alcatraz

Ethel Rosenberg, executed at Sing Sing prison near her native New York City for conspiracy to commit espionage

Julius Rosenberg, executed at Sing Sing prison near his native New York City for conspiracy to commit espionage

Al Sarant, stole radar secrets at Army Signal Corps lab in New Jersey, then he and his mistress abandoned their families for the protection of his Soviet masters in 1950

Andrew Roth, Office of Naval Intelligence liaison officer with United States Department of State

Saville Sax college friend of Theodore Hall assisted with Hall's disclosure to the Soviets of Los Alamos research and development

**Silvermaster group**

Nathan Gregory Silvermaster, Chief Planning Technician, Procurement Division, United States Department of the Treasury; Chief Economist, War Assets Administration; Director of the Labor Division, Farm Security Administration; Board of Economic Warfare; Reconstruction Finance Corporation Department of Commerce

Helen Silvermaster (wife)

Schlomer Adler, United States Department of the Treasury

Norman Chandler Bursler, United States Department of Justice

Anti-Trust Division

Frank Coe, Assistant Director, Division of Monetary Research, Treasury Department; Special Assistant to the United States Ambassador in London; Assistant to the Executive Director, Board of Economic Warfare; Assistant Administrator, Foreign Economic Administration

Lauchlin Currie, Administrative Assistant to President Roosevelt; Deputy Administrator of Foreign Economic Administration; Special Representative to China

Bela Gold, Assistant Head of Program Surveys, Bureau of Agricultural Economics, Agriculture Department; Senate Subcommittee on War Mobilization; Office of Economic Programs in Foreign Economic Administration

Sonia Steinman Gold, Division of Monetary Research U.S. Treasury Department; U.S. House of Representatives Select Committee on Interstate Migration; U.S. Bureau of Employment Security

Irving Kaplan, Foreign Funds Control and Division of Monetary Research, United States Department of the Treasury Foreign Economic Administration; chief advisor to the Military Government of Germany

George Silverman, civilian Chief Production Specialist, Material Division, United States Army Air Forces Air Staff, War Department, Pentagon

William Henry Taylor, Assistant Director of the Middle East Division of Monetary Research, United States Department of Treasury

William Ullman, delegate to United Nations Charter meeting and Bretton Woods conference; Division of Monetary Research, Department of Treasury; Material and Services Division, Air Corps Headquarters, Pentagon

Anatole Volkov

Harry Dexter White, Assistant Secretary of the Treasury; Head of the International Monetary Fund

Sound and Myrna groups

Solomon Adler, United States Department of the Treasury

Cedric Belfrage, journalist; British Security Coordination

Elizabeth Bentley courier messenger for Communist spy rings on the American East Coast in the 30s, testified about her activities in hearings in the 40s and 50s

Frank Coe, Assistant Director, Division of Monetary Research, Treasury Department; Special Assistant to the United States Ambassador in London; Assistant to the Executive Director, Board of Economic Warfare; Assistant Administrator, Foreign Economic Administration

Lauchlin Currie, Administrative Assistant to President Roosevelt; Deputy Administrator of Foreign Economic Administration; Special Representative to China

Rae Elson, an active Communist, and courier of the CPUSA underground, was chosen by Joseph Katz to replace Bentley at the Soviet front organization, U.S. Shipping and Service Corporation.

Frederick V. Field, Executive Secretary American Peace Mobilization

Edward Fitzgerald, War Production Board

Charles Flato, Board of Economic Warfare; Civil Liberties Subcommittee, Senate Committee on Education and Labor

Eva Getzov, Jewish Welfare Board

Bela Gold, Bureau of Intelligence, Assistant Head of Program Surveys, Bureau of Agricultural Economics, Agriculture Department; Senate Subcommittee on War Mobilization; Office of Economic Programs in Foreign Economic Administration

Sonia Steinman Gold, Division of Monetary Research U.S. Treasury Department; U.S. House of Representatives Select Committee on Interstate Migration; U.S. Bureau of Employment Security

Irving Goldman, Office of the Coordinator of Inter-American Affairs

Jacob Golos, the "main pillar" of the NKVD intelligence network in the U.S., died in the arms of comrade Elizabeth Bentley

Gerald Graze, United States Civil Service Commission;

Department of Defense, U.S. Navy official

Stanley Graze, United States Department of State intelligence

Michael Greenberg, Board of Economic Warfare; Administrative Division, Enemy Branch, Foreign Economic Administration; United States Department of State

Joseph Gregg, Office of the Coordinator of Inter-American Affairs; United States Department of State

Maurice Halperin, Chief of Latin American Division, Research and Analysis section, Office of Strategic Services; United States Department of State

Julius Joseph, Far Eastern section (Japanese Intelligence) Office of Strategic Services

Irving Kaplan, United States Department of the Treasury Foreign Economic Administration; United Nations Division of Economic Stability and Development; Chief Advisor to the Military Government of Germany

Joseph Katz

Charles Kramer, Senate Subcommittee on War Mobilization; Office of Price Administration; National Labor Relations Board; Senate Subcommittee on Wartime Health and Education; Agricultural Adjustment Administration; Civil Liberties Subcommittee, Senate Committee on Education and Labor; Senate Labor and Public Welfare Committee; Democratic National Committee

Duncan Lee, counsel to General William Donovan, head of Office of Strategic Services

Bernice Levin, Office of Emergency Management; Office of Production Management

Helen Lowry, (Elza Akhmerova), Akhmerov wife, American-born and raised, Soviet citizen

Harry Magdoff, Chief of the Control Records Section of War Production Board and Office of Emergency Management; Bureau of Research and Statistics, WTB; Tools Division, War Production Board; Bureau of Foreign and Domestic Commerce, United States Department of Commerce; Statistics Division Works Progress Administration

Jenny Levy Miller, Chinese Government Purchasing Commission

Robert Miller, Office of the Coordinator of Inter-American Affairs; Near Eastern Division United States Department of State

Ezra Moscrip, Nuclear Physicist who worked on the Manhattan Project. Accused of selling secrets to the USSR during World War II. Found dead in NYC apartment in 1945

Willard Park, Assistant Chief of the Economic Analysis Section, Office of the Coordinator of Inter-American Affairs; United Nations Relief and Rehabilitation Administration

Victor Perlo, chief of the Aviation Section of the War Production Board; head of branch in Research Section, Office of Price Administration Department of Commerce; Division of Monetary Research Department of Treasury; Brookings Institution, head of Perlo group

Mary Price, stenographer for Walter Lippmann of the New York Herald

Bernard Redmont, head of the Foreign News Bureau Office of the Coordinator of Inter-American Affairs

William Remington, War Production Board; Office of Emergency Management, convicted for perjury, killed in prison

Ruth Rivkin, United Nations Relief and Rehabilitation Administration

Allan Rosenberg, Board of Economic Warfare; Chief of the Economic Institution Staff, Foreign Economic Administration; Civil Liberties Subcommittee, Senate Committee on Education and Labor; Railroad Retirement Board; Councel to the Secretary of the National Labor Relations Board

Bernard Schuster

Greg Silvermaster, Chief Planning Technician, Procurement Division, United States Department of the Treasury; Chief Economist, War Assets Administration; Director of the Labor Division, Farm Security Administration; Board of Economic Warfare; Reconstruction Finance Corporation Department of Commerce

John Spivak, journalist

William Taylor, Assistant Director of Monetary Research, United States Department of Treasury

Helen Tenney, Office of Strategic Services

Lee Tenney, Balkan Division Office of Strategic Services

Lud Ullman, delegate to United Nations Charter meeting and Bretton Woods conference; Division of Monetary Research, Department of Treasury; Material and Services Division, Air Corps Headquarters, Pentagon

David Weintraub, United States Department of State; head of the Office of Foreign Relief and Rehabilitation Operations; United Nations Relief and Rehabilitation Administration (UNRRA); United Nations Division of Economic Stability and Development

Donald Wheeler, Office of Strategic Services Research and Analysis division

Anatoly Gorsky, (Anatoly Veniaminovich Gorsky, A. V. Gorsky), "Vadim", former rezident of the MGB USSR in Washington

Olga Pravdina, former employee of the Ministry of Trade, wife of "Sergei," the rezident in New York

Vladimir Pravdin, "Sergei", Tass, former rezident of the MGB USSR in New York

Mikhail A. Shaliapin [Shalyapin], "Stock"

Gaik Badelovich Ovakimian, former rezident of the MGB USSR in New York

Iskhak Abdulovich Akhmerov, "Albert" – former Illegal Rezident of the MGB USSR in New York

Arthur Gerald Steinberg, United States Office of Scientific Research and Development

Michael Straight, speechwriter for President Franklin Roosevelt

Lev Vasilevsky, KGB Illegal Rezident Mexico City

John Anthony Walker US Navy senior enlisted man who spied for the Soviet Union for decades, enlisting family and friends to do so as well

**Ware group**

Whittaker Chambers, Department of State, testified against Alger Hiss

Henry Collins, National Recovery Administration; Department of Agriculture

John Herrmann, CPUSA operative and courier, eventually drank himself to death in Mexico

Alger Hiss, Department of State, sentenced to 5 years for perjury

Donald Hiss, Department of State, younger brother of Alger Hiss

Victor Perlo, became spymaster of Perlo group during World War II

George Silverman, Harvard-educated statistician who gave secret Pentagon documents to Nathan Silvermaster group during World War II

Harry Dexter White, Assistant Secretary of the Treasury; head of the International Monetary Fund which he helped establish along with the World Bank

Ruby Weil, American communist who assisted in plot to murder Leon Trotsky

Bill Weisband, United States Army Signals Security Agency

Enos Wicher, professor at Columbia University who also worked at Columbia's Division of War Research; stepfather of Barnard College recruitress and State Department spy Flora Wovschin

**KGB Illegals**

Rudolf Abel, aka William Fischer, Illegal Rezident in the 1950s

A. I. Akhmerov, "Albert" – former Illegal Rezident of the MGB USSR in New York

**GRU (Soviet military intelligence)**

Arvid Jacobson

Karl groupDavid Carpenter (David Zimmerman)

Noel Field, United States Department of State

Harold Glasser, Director, Division of Monetary Research, United States Department of the Treasury; United Nations Relief and Rehabilitation Administration; War Production Board; Advisor on North African Affairs Committee; United States Treasury Representative to the Allied High Commission in Italy

Alger Hiss, United States Department of State, sentenced to 5 years for perjury

Donald Hiss, United States Department of State; United States Department of Labor; United States Department of the Interior

Victor Perlo, chief of the Aviation Section of the War Production Board; head of branch in Research Section, Office of Price Administration Department of Commerce; Division of Monetary Research Department of Treasury; Brookings Institution, head of Perlo group

J. Peters

William Ward Pigman, National Bureau of Standards; Labor and Public Welfare Committee

Vincent Reno, mathematician at United States Army Aberdeen Proving Ground

George Silverman, Director of the Bureau of Research and Information Services, US Railroad Retirement Board; Economic Adviser and Chief of Analysis and Plans, Assistant Chief of Air Staff, Material and Services, War Department

Julian Wadleigh, United States Department of State

Harry Dexter White, Assistant Secretary of the Treasury; Head of the International Monetary Fund

Viktor Vasilevish Sveshchnikov, United States War Department

**Portland ring**

Konon Molody (aka Gordon Lonsdale)

Juliet Poyntz

Fred Rose (politician), Canadian Member of Parliament, first elected from the Labour-Progressive Party (Canada) 1943

Milton Schwartz

**Sorge ring**

Chen Han-seng

Hotsumi Ozaki

Agnes Smedley

William Spiegel

Lydia Stahl

Joseph Benjamin Stenbuck

Irving Charles Velson, Brooklyn Navy Yard; American Labor Party candidate for New York State Senate

Flora Wovschin, NKVD operative in U.S. State Department, comrade of Marion Davis Berdecio and Judith Coplon from their days at Columbia University
    Vasily Zarubin, husband of Elizabeth Zubilin
    Elizabeth Zubilin, recruiter in U.S. of whom Pavel Sudoplatov, head of NKVD Fourth Directorate said, "In developing J. Robert Oppenheimer as a source, Elizabeth Zubilin was essential."

**Hitler was a KGB asset ?**

### *Spy Code by Mikhail Kryzhanovsky*

1. No mercy, no ideology, no emotions.
2. Intuition is nothing but the ability to watch and analyze.
3. No evidence is evidence in itself. .
4. Distrust is a mother of security.
5. Never look as if you are sizing up the person — that's a sign that gives away cops and spies.
6. Don't start first if you don't know the rules.
7. The way you act is the way you think — behavior is a system of codes (information) which could be calculated by the enemy. Watch your face — that's a shop window.
8. Think fast, talk slow.
9. Avoid self-programming and never think bad about yourself.
10. Don't smoke, drink or take drugs if it's not necessary; spare your stomach from very hot or cold food or drinks; avoid too much noise and light.
11. Don't be shy to lie — the more you lie the more people respect you.
12. Let people talk out and "empty their brains" — then load your information.
13. People never change — everybody wants to get pleasure and avoid pain.
14. "He knew too much" means "He talked too much."

15. Never ask extra questions — wait. Wait and the object will get used to you and open himself — nobody can stay tense for long.
16. Lonely people live longer in espionage business.
17. "No exit" situation is the one you don't like or don't understand.
18. Avoid:
- personal enemies (they fix negative information on you)
- silent types (they notice and think too much)
- other professionals (they'll blow your identity)
- extra stress (it damages your heart and blood vessels and that kills your brain and your ability to think )
- talking too much CIA or KGB ?

**They might send you anywhere and you must know what's special about major countries and their people.**

*United States of America*
Americans' lives revolve around work. Keep your distance when conversing with them, don't stare – it's a very rude behavior. They don't hesitate to say "no", are opportunistic and willing to take chances, future oriented and consistent. Say "please" and "thank you" as often as you can. They are often uncomfortable with silence. Always be on time and meet deadlines. Meetings are generally informal and relaxed in manner, but serious in content (participation is expected – a quiet person may be viewed as not prepared). They appreciate and are impressed by numbers (statistics). They often begin negotiations with unacceptable conditions. Persistence is another characteristic – there is a prevailing belief that there is always a solution. In a business setting the person extending the invitation to a meal pays for it. Most government employees are not allowed to accept gifts. Cash gifts are never appropriate.

*Russia*
Russians are transactional and do not need to establish long-standing personal relationships. Most of them don't trust people who are "all business". heavy drinkers.

*United Kingdom*

England is a kingdom within the United Kingdom, and ignoring the subdivisions of the United Kingdom and referring to the whole as "England" is insulting to the inhabitants of Wales, Scotland and Northern Ireland. Look reserved, but usually they are friendly and helpful to foreigners, especially women. It doesn't matter what country you are from – try to be a 100% gentleman. Don't insult the Royal Family or show great interest in their private lives. Don't ask personal questions and don't talk about money. Don't shout or be loud in public places, except Hyde Park.

*Ireland*

Asking people whether they are Catholic or Protestant is insensitive. Very famous for drinking strong alcohol (whisky), but they respect reserved behavior. Do not stare at people – that means you want to fight (for a man), or you want to kiss (for a woman). Don't rush the Irish. Creative and calm in crisis, but poor in long-range planning.

*Netherland*

They are extremely adept at dealing with foreigners (the most successful traders in Europe; they are direct, giving straight "yes" or "no". Do not discuss money or prices or ask personal questions.

*Norway*

Norwegians are excellent time managers and direct communicators ; conservative and deliberate speakers who do not appreciate being rushed. They are scrupulous about honesty in communication. Appearing overly friendly may be viewed as weakness. Maintaining eye contact while speaking is interpreted as sincerity.

*Denmark*

Danes prefer to get down to business quickly; communication is frank and direct.

*Canada*

Canadians are more reserved than Americans. They can be agreeable and they are often gracious hosts though thy don't have difficulty in saying "no". Decisions are not rushed and a certain amount of caution is advised. When in Quebec, learn a little French – people greatly appreciate that. Do not compare Canada with the United States. Do not take sides in debates about contentious national issues (status of Quebec, the place of French and English languages in Canada). Don't eat while walking or standing on the street in Quebec.

*Germany*

The Third Reich is a sensitive subject; Nazi symbolism and gestures are illegal in Germany, as is denying the Holocaust. It is impolite to ask how someone will vote in a specific matter. Socially, Germans lean toward conservatism and conformism. Germans are uneasy with uncertainty, ambiguity and unquantifiable risk and put heavy emphasis on careful planning, consideration and consultation. Do not rush proceedings or apply pressure. They rarely change their decisions. Never put your hands in your pockets when talking to someone. Don't point your index figure to your own head – this is an insult. They are hard bargainers. Decision making is slow with thorough analysis of all facts. Don't be offended if someone corrects your behavior – policing each other is seen as a social duty. Don't chew gum in public.

*France*

French cherish their culture, history, language and food. Not finishing the wine is considered very rude as it indicates that the host has served a wine of poor quality. Many of them speak and understand English, but prefer not to use it. Don't discuss personal life with business people. French communication style is direct, questioning and probing. The French get down to business quickly, but make decisions slowly (they are leaders in economic planning). Don't ask personal questions related to occupation, family or children unless you have a well-established friendship. Try to demonstrate some knowledge of history, politics and French culture. The French do not tell or like to hear jokes, instead they prefer intelligent and satirical real life stories. "OK" gesture means "zero" or "worthless" in France.

*Japan*

Nodding is very important. Silence is a natural and expected form of non-verbal communication. Sit erect . Any degree of knowledge of Japanese culture is greatly appreciated. Avoid saying "no'. Drinking is a group activity; never say "no' when offered a drink. At dinner wait for the toast before you drink. "Maybe" means "no". A smile or laughter from a Japanese may mean they are feeling nervous or uncomfortable, and not necessarily happy. Business cards should be given and accepted with both hands. It is expected that the cards will immediately be inspected and admired, then placed on the table in front of the receiver for the duration of the meeting. After the meeting, cards should be stored respectfully and should never be placed in back pocket. . Silence is considered a virtue, so never interrupt or break the silence.

*Kuwait*

You must be patient since impatience is viewed as criticism of the culture. Kuwaitis respect education, so carefully mention if you have an advanced degree, especially if it's from a prestigious university. Meetings may be interrupted if they interfere with prayer times. Kuwaitis are event rather than time-driven (the event of getting together is more important). Decisions are reached slowly. Repeating your main points indicates you are telling the truth.

*China*

The Chinese are not keen on physical contact – especially when doing business. Above all, be patient and never show anger. You must be willing to show compromise. Banking contacts are very important. Take time to build relationships. People are very superstitious – don't mention failure, poverty or death. Speaking even a few words of Chinese is greatly appreciated.

*Singapore*

Singaporeans tend to get right down to business in meetings and make decisions quickly. Singapore has strict regulations which carry stiff fines, possible jail sentences or even death. You should never do the following: jaywalk, smoke in public or in air-conditioned buildings (except country clubs), enter the country with drugs, litter, or import, manufacture, sell or use chewing gum. Avoid discussing religion or politics.

*Taiwan*

The people of Taiwan value hard work, patience, friendliness, but they are hard bargainers – be patient.

*Korea*

The number 4 is considered unlucky, so gifts should not be given in multiples of four. Giving 7 of an item is considered lucky.

*Thailand*

Touching someone on the foot is a taboo; touching someone's head requires immediate apology. Kissing in the streets and any public display of affection are considered rude, though Thais are relatively liberal-minded in matters of sexuality. Thais hold their king in very high regard. Currency, postage stamps, magazine covers and other items with the king's image are never tossed to the ground, and even licking the back of a postage stamp is considered disrespectful.

*Spain*

Be careful discussing independent movements within Spain, religion and political issues surrounding fascism and nationalism. Spain is among the most liberal countries in Europe. The way you present yourself is of critical importance; trust and personal relationships too. Avoid confrontation – Spaniards do not like to publicly admit that they are incorrect. You may be interrupted while you are speaking, this is not an insult, it means the person is interested in what you are saying. Spaniards do not like to "lose face", so they will not necessarily say they do not understand something, though they are very thorough.

*Austria*

First impressions are important and you will be judged on your clothing and demeanour. Austrians are suspicious of hyperbole, promises that sound too good to be true, or displays of emotion.

*Italy*

Cultural achievements is Italy's greatest source of pride. The family is the most important affiliation in Italy. Maintain eye contact while talking, otherwise Italians might think you are hiding something. Establish personal (profitable) relationships with Italians. Although written agendas are frequently provided , they may not be followed – they serve as a jumping off point .Decisions are often made and agreed to privately before meetings, which are meant for a free flow of ideas and let everyone have their say. Decisions that are made and agreed to may never be implemented, and they are often based on how you are viewed. Hard drinking is not appreciated – even mild intoxication is considered ill-mannered. Italians enjoy a lot of good humor. Refrain from asking personal questions. When visiting a home in Italy it is impolite to remove one's coat until asked. Complimenting on food and asking for more is regarded as a very polite thing to do and every host is expected to prepare food in abundance.

*Saudi Arabia*

Since Saudis will judge you on appearances, dress and present yourself well. Never inquire about a Saudi's wife. Decisions are made slowly and are easily overturned; the society is extremely bureaucratic and most decisions require several layers of approval. .

*Egypt*

Expect to be offered coffee or tea whenever you meet someone, declining the offer is viewed as rejecting the person. Egyptians judge people on appearances, so you must wear good quality conservative clothes. They believe direct eye contact is a sign of honesty, so be ready for disconcertingly intense stares. Decisions are reached after great deliberation, the society is extremely bureaucratic.They don't like confrontation and abhor saying "no"; if they do not respond, it means "no".

*South Africa*

South Africans are transactional and do not need to establish long-standing personal relationships before conducting business. They avoid confrontation and often use metaphors and sports analogies to demonstrate a point. Personal relationships are important. Do not interrupt South African while they are speaking; they strive for consensus and win-win situations. Start negotiations with realistic figure – they do not like haggling over the price.

*Switzerland*
Proud of their neutrality, have a deep-rooted respect for savings and wealth. Take punctuality very seriously.

*Sweden*
Patriotism is important to Swedes who are very proud of their nation, towns and regions. Take punctuality very seriously. Swedes are factual, practical, precise, reserved and get to the point quickly. Be clear and concise in detailing what you expect from them. Knowledge about Sweden's economy , high standard of living, sports, architecture, history is appreciated. Do not criticize Swedish lifestyle, sexual habits, suicide rate, prices.

*Australia*
Have no difficulty is saying "no". It may be impolite to remark on Australia's history as penal colony. They enjoy easy-going lifestyle and are generally friendly and relaxed. The "V" sign is considered to be very vulgar. Australians respect people with strong opinions, even if they don't agree. Avoid discussions about the treatment of the aboriginal people. Don't comment on anyone's accent – accents often distinguish social class.

*Indonesia*
They value loyalty to the family and friends above all else. Indonesia as a whole is viewed by its people as an extended family with the president, schoolmasters and leaders of business enterprises referred to as "fathers" by the public. They love to bargain. Avoid disagreement and arguments with Indonesians, do not apply pressure or be confrontational. Civil servants are respected – be very respectful to government workers. Most Indonesians are Muslims and consume no liquor or pork.

*Belgium*
Hard work, appreciation for culture, strong family systems. Accept any drink offered by your host and don't ask for a drink not offered. Belgians are thrifty and do not appreciate waste – finish all the food on your plate. Avoid discussing personal matters or linguistic divisions with them. Do not flaunt wealth. Do not as questions about private lives.

*Argentina*

The "OK" and "thumbs up" gestures are considered vulgar. Personal relationships are important and must be developed before business is done. Don't compare Argentina with the United States or with Brazil, which is considered rival. Avoid talking about Great Britain or the Falkland Islands - these are sensitive subjects to many Argentines. Be careful when discussing the Peron years – people either love or hate the Perons. Although Argentines may be very vocal about politics and religion, avoid adding your opinions to these discussions. They do not like publicly admitting they are incorrect. If a favor is done for you, you will eventually be called upon to re-pay it. They prefer face-to-face meetings rather than by telephone or in writing, which are seen as impersonal. Once a relationship has been developed, their loyalty will be to you rather than to the government you represent.

*Mexico*

Strong sense of fatalism. Social stratifications are well-defined. .The status of your hotel accommodations, the quality of your clothes and watch, and whether or not you arrive in a chauffeured limousine will be critically appraised by Mexican counterparts. Be persistent, don't give up if your meetings are postponed or canceled; if you give up, Mexicans might assume that you weren't serious in the first place. Any attempt to speak Spanish is appreciated; Mexicans are very proud of their independence and have a strong sense of national identity and pride. Never compare the way things are done in Mexico with the way they are done in USA.

*India*

Industrial leader with millions of poor people. "I will try" means "no". Never show anger – if you lose your temper , you "lose face" and prove you are unworthy of trust. Delays are to be expected, especially dealing with the government. Indians expect concessions and it's acceptable to expect concessions in return for those you made. It's inappropriate for a man to make any comment about a woman's appearance. Asking a person to a social event (restaurant) means that the person offering the invite will be paying for everything.

| CIA | KGB |
|---|---|
| Cuts corners to save money on intelligence. | No limitations. |
| Poor professional training and knowledge. | KGB was famous for brilliant analysts. |
| "Country inside country." | Mostly patriots. |
| Results first. | Security first. |
| Use people and get rid of them. | Respect your sources. |
| Promise and forget. | Promise and do it. |
| Saw Russia as #1 enemy. | Saw US as #1 enemy. |
| Money first. | Job first. |
| Alcohol. | Alcohol. |
| "We are the best." | "No, we are the best". |
| Unreformable. | A fluid structure. |

## KGB

Since 1991, the KGB has been re-named the SVR (Russian Intelligence Service), but it has basically the same structure.

Structure
KGB Chief and his Deputies
Directorates:

"R" — operational planning and analysis

"K": external counter-intelligence

"S": illegal spies

"T": scientific and technical intelligence, acquisition of Western strategic, military and industrial technology.

"RI": intelligence assessment

"RT": operations within the Soviet Union

"OT": operational technical support

"I": computer services

"P": political intelligence

Geographic Departments.

Services:

"A": disinformation, covert actions to influence foreign nations and governments

"R": radio communications with overseas stations

"A" of the 8th Chief Directorate (cryptographic services)

KGB station abroad:

KGB Resident (Chief of the station).

"PR" line: political, economic and military strategic intelligence

"KR" line: counterintelligence and security

"X" line: scientific and technological intelligence

"N" line: illegal spies' support

"EM" line: émigrés

"SK" line: Soviet colony in the country

Embassy security officer

"OT" officer — operational technical support

"Impulse" station — monitoring of radio communications of surveillance teams

"RP" line officer: SIGINT

"I" line officer — computers

Cipher clerk

Radio operator

KGB inside humor:
"Recruit a woman if you can't recruit anybody else."
"You can lose nothing and you can find nothing inside the KGB."
"Never make friends inside the KGB."
"Before lunch we fight hunger, after lunch we fight sleep."
"The law stops here."

KGB slang sounds funny too: "music" (listening device), "Bible"(a book with listening device hidden inside), "gods"(officers who worked with informants inside churches and sects), "sailor" (informant — informant's KGB registration card was crossed by a red stripe), "crust" (KGB ID), "To take a skin off" (to take information from the informant), "to spin information" (to "enrich" information with false facts), "lime-tree" false information). There are still stereotypes about the KGB, like "KGB knows everything" or "KGB never arrests innocent citizens," or "KGB officers take special pills and that's why they are never drunk." Yes, KGB officers drink vodka on weekends and sometimes in the offices with regular Russian appetizers like smoked sausage or fish, caviar and pickles, but it's a rare thing to see somebody really drunk. They drink mostly to ease tension from the job and social isolation. If you don't drink alcohol with your colleagues it means disrespect and is not very good for your promotion. They take no pills and are just accustomed to regulate themselves.

The KGB business goes in cycles and it's like any other bureaucratic government agency — July and August are "dead" months (vacations) as well as November and December (planning and waiting for promotion). The crazy busy months are January, February, March and June, because the departments and divisions chiefs try to do most of the job (especially recruitment) that was planned for the whole year. If you still don't do anything it's not a problem but if you miss the recruitment targets, you are in trouble. First, it's not professional and even your friends won't understand; second, it's a problem now for somebody else, because if you haven't met the recruitment target somebody has to recruit instead of you — and in a rush. .

KGB officers, due to professional demands, are physically fit, intelligent, well educated, have no mental problems and know how to talk and charm people — that's the art of recruitment. All these qualities create a big problem for married men (99% are married) because women like them. Almost every officer has a lover, but divorce is out of question. First, it's bad for your career, second, you and your bosses have a terrible headache, because if you divorce and want to marry again, they have to check this woman — she must have "clean" biography: no criminals in the family, no relatives abroad, no mentally ill family members and she has to be normal too. In earlier years, every KGB officer was a CPSU (Communist Party of the Soviet Union) member and there were no political problems between the Party leaders and KGB chiefs. Still, there existed a super-secret Special Investigation Department in Moscow which was responsible for investigation of espionage or other criminal activity by senior Party members or government officials.

## CIA

The Reagan transition team for the CIA (November, 1980) reported the following:

**"The fundamental problem confronting American security is the current dangerous condition of the Central Intelligence Agency and of national intelligence collection generally. The failure of American intelligence collection has been at the heart of faulty defense planning and misdirected foreign policy."**

The team pointed out to the following intelligence failures:

- the general and continuing failure to predict the actual size and scope of the Soviet military effort and military sector of the Russian GNP
- the consistent gross misstatement of Soviet global objectives
- the wholesale failure to understand or attempt to counteract

Soviet disinformation and propaganda

- the general failure to explain the characteristics of Soviet conventional weapon systems and vessels — for example the new Russian guided missile cruises
- the wholesale failure to understand and predict the nature of the so-called wars of national liberation in Africa and Central and South America
- the consistent miscalculation regarding the effect of and general apology for massive technology transfer from West to the East
- the apparent internal failure of counterintelligence generally.

The team went on to observe."The unhealthy symbiosis between the CIA and the Department of State is the chief underlying cause of the security position of the United States. The next Director of the Central Intelligence Agency ... will be told repeatedly by virtually everyone in policy positions at the Agency that the CIA is a highly professional, non-political agency that produces 'objective' intelligence. Those assertions are arrant nonsense. In part out of mutual drive for individual and corporate self-preservation, the CIA has become an elitist organization which engenders unshakable loyalty among its staff. The National Intelligence Estimate process is itself a bureaucratic game. These failures are of such enormity, that they cannot help but suggest to any objective observer that the agency itself is compromised to an unprecedented extent and that its paralysis is attributable to causes more sinister than incompetence."

## MOSSAD

1. Very effective method of non-stop 24/7 monitoring of all Arab terrorists leaders' movements all over the world. Don't you think they know where Osama Bin-Laden is? — if MOSSAD had informants among his aides before, it has them now.
2. Unlimited practice of political murders — which means MOSSAD has no idea how to recruit and work with Arab agents (monitoring is a passive tool).
3. MOSSAD has been super-active at the United Nations, with

zero effect — 99% of the UN delegates vote against Israel on every issue.

My Israeli colleagues have some unfortunate qualities: they promote an unprecedented level of PR according to which every MOSSAD officer is a genius and each MOSSAD Director is "Mr. Intelligence." MOSSAD unfortunately soiled its reputation in the international espionage community after the case of the exceptionally unprofessional John Pollard. The following morality tale emphasizes the first rule of recruitment — do not recruit psychos.

John Pollard was born in 1954 in Texas to a Jewish family. He studied at Stanford University and being a schizophrenic and drug abuser, claimed he was a colonel in the Israeli army and a MOSSAD spy. After Stanford the US Navy hired him in 1979 as a civilian intelligence analyst at Naval Operational Surveillance and Intelligence Center, the Naval Intelligence Support Center and the Naval Investigative Center.In 1984 they brought him into the Anti-Terrorism Alert Center where he gained access to the whole federal intelligence system and a high level of clearance known as SCI or Sensitive Compartmented Information, and a special "courier card" that opened the CIA, FBI, State Department and National Security Agency restricted archives for him.

In May 1984, through a New York businessman, he was introduced to Israeli Air Force colonel Aviem Sella. Pollard told him that he had positive proof that the USA, the only Israel's ally, friend and sponsor, was not sharing all the intelligence data it should with Israel, and Pollard was angry with the US and willing to help his historic motherland. (In truth, although Israel does not share much with the US, Israel was receiving full political, economic and military support from the US plus $3 billion a year at that time — and even more in recent years.) The report about the "walk-in" volunteer was passed to Rafi Eitan, the LACAM (Israeli military technology espionage agency) chief, and in a month Pollard was recruited. For a year Pollard was supplying Israel with top secret documents, including satellite reconnaissance photographs which were of a special interest to LACAM. The documents were going straight to Prime Minister Shimon Pres, Foreign Minister Yitzhak Shamir and Defense Minister Yitzhak Rabin.

Finally on November 21, 1985 the FBI went after him. In a chase, he made it into the Israeli embassy in Washington, DC, but the MOSSAD officers threw him out. He may spend the rest of his life in jail. So far President George Bush and President Bill Clinton have refused the multiple Israeli requests to pardon him.

Since 2000 MOSSAD has advertised its recruitment of collection officers (a concept which is unthinkable for the KGB).

### Ministry of State Security (MSS), China.

China's MSS aggressively targets the US high tech sector heavily concentrated in Silicon Valley. Cover for Beijing's espionage includes the 1,500 Chinese diplomats, 15,000 Chinese students who arrive here each year and 2, 700 visiting delegations each year and the US correspondents of the major Chinese newspapers, including The People's Daily and Xinhua News Agency. (Altogether the MSS has established "branches" in 170 cities in nearly 50 countries all over the world). Here what communist China is doing in the United States.

1998 was a very special year. We got 4 (four) cases of suspected Chinese espionage against the United States dating back to the 1980s. The most serious case involved China's alleged acquisition of key information about our nation's most advanced miniaturized US nuclear warhead, the W-88, as well as serious security breaches at the Department of Energy (DOE) Los Alamos Laboratory between 1984 and 1988. In 1997 Dr. Peter Lee, who worked in Los Alamos on classified projects relating to the use of lasers to stimulate nuclear detonations, was convicted for passing classified national defense information to China's representatives. In 1999, FBI arrested Wen Lee, a Taiwan-born Chinese American scientist, who downloaded critical nuclear weapons codes, called legacy codes, from a classified computer system at Los Alamos to an unclassified system accessible to anyone with the proper password. Same year the President's Foreign Intelligence Advisory Board presented a report saying that DOE "is a dysfunctional bureaucracy that has proven it is incapable of reforming itself".

China is striving to acquire advanced American technology of any sort, whether for military or civilian purposes, as part of its government program to improve its entire economic infrastructure – a direct threat to our national security. They are mostly interested in astronautics, information technology, laser technology, automation technology, energy technology, new materials. Watch, if you have to deal with China Aerospace Corporation (CASC) and its Hong Kong subsidiary China Aerospace International Holdings, China National Nuclear Corporation (CNNC), China North Industries Group (NORINCO), Aviation Industries Corporation of China (AVIC), China Nanchang Aircraft Manufacturing Company, China National South Aero-Engine and Machinery Company, Qinghua University Nuclear Research Institute, China International Trade and Investment Company (CITIC), Polytechnologies Corporation, China Great Wall Industry Corporation, China State Shipbuilding Corporation (CSSC), China Ocean Shipping Company (COSCO).

China is trying to steal from us information in the following areas of military concern:
1. Biological warfare. Gene researches (bioengineering) that could have biological warfare application.
2. Space technology. Satellites with remote sensing capabilities, which could be used for military reconnaissance, as well as space launch vehicles.
3. Military information technology. Intelligent computers, optoelectronics, image processing for weather forecasting; the production of submicron integrated circuits on 8-inch silicon wafers. These programs could lead to the development of military communications systems; command, control communications and intelligence systems; advances in military software development.

4. Laser weapons. Pulse-power techniques, plasma technology and laser spectroscopy, all of which are useful in the development of laser weapons.
   5. Automation technology. Computer-integrated manufacturing systems and robotics. Electronics, machinery, space, chemistry, telecommunications.
   6. Nuclear weapons.
   7. Exotic materials. Optoelectronic information materials, structural materials, special function materials, composites, rare-earth metals, new energy compound materials that could advance the development of military aircraft.

### " *Illegal* " *spies.*

When I talk about "the best," I mean the highest intelligence level — illegal spies, intelligence operatives who are secretly deployed abroad and covertly operate there under assumed names and well-documented cover stories, masquerading as native citizens. It's very important if you get , for example, original birth certificate of American citizen, who died (at young age preferably) or any records and documents on him(birth, wedding, death, any IDs, etc) .

*The process of training and "installing" such officer is rather complex and includes:*

a) Special training. Foreign language, general, political and special (espionage and counter-espionage) knowledge of the target country; personal cover story — new biography, special technical devices, recruitment methods). Up to three years.
   b) Illegal probation period abroad. A trip abroad through intermediate countries with numerous changes of passports and cover stories, jobs, personal connections. Then he gets to the target country, stays there for another 1-2 years and goes back to his country for additional training and correction of cover story — actually, it's his first combat assignment. The most important

part of this assignment is to check the reliability of the cover story and documents; the cover story has to be reinforced with new and old true facts, like short-term studies at universities or professional training courses).

c) Intermediate legislation. On his way back the officer could stay in an intermediate country for another 1-2 years, make contacts with business, scientists, government employees, celebrities.

d) Basic legislation. Officer comes to the target country, obtains genuine documents, gets a job which allows him to travel and talk to many people, recruit informants thus creating an illegal station.

The illegal is usually supplied with a variety of cover documents to make him "invisible" for counter-intelligence — some are used only to cross the borders on the way to a target country, others — to live there, other documents — only for travel to "third countries" to meet with officers of legal or illegal stations or to be used in case of urgent recall to home country (in that case the illegal is supposed to transit at least two or three countries). His further activity depends on how professional counter-espionage service is working in the country.

He could fail in his mission also because of:
- poor training and low quality documents
- neglecting security rules.
- one mistake in pronunciation can give you away
- treason (traitor-informant or a "mole" inside his own service)
- low personal security level (while working with sources)


**My illegal espionage operation "Kremlin"**

My KGB intelligence officer career came to an end when USSR collapsed in 1991. Next 2 years ,as SBU (Ukrainian Security) illegal spy under cover of political analyst, I worked in Moscow (operation "Kremlin"). My job was to get into Russian President Boris Yeltsin "inner circle" and influence his decisions, extremely anti-Ukrainian at the time. I met people who knew Yeltsin well, like Russian Parliament Constitutional Committee Chairman Rumyantsev and one of Yeltsin's photographers, who asked me to work for him.

In February 1992, I could kill Yeltsin if ordered so by Ukrainian President Kravchuk.

As a former KGB "Nabat" (anti-terror) group sniper I knew perfectly well how they protected Yeltsin. Besides, in 1986 I joined A. Gromyko, Chairman of the USSR Supreme Soviet (actually, the USSR President), security team during his visit to Gorky city and it was a big experience too. I was working alone, though you have to send three groups for operation like this one : surveillance (with optics and radios), action (includes snipers, explosives technicians or staged accidents specialists), and security (these people neutralize bodyguards, witnesses and other people who could interrupt the action; they complete the action if the action group fails; and they can neutralize the action group later, if planned so;

they "cover" the safe retreat of action group and "cut" the chase.

Operation was in progress until there was a leak and Yeltsin got information about it. In 1992 Russia and Ukraine signed a Treaty to stop mutual espionage. President Kravchuk ordered to kill me as a witness of his dirty politics. I moved to Poland and then, in 1995, to USA.

CIA decided to copy "Kremlin" in Washington, DC.

## SVR (Russian Intelligence) operation "Hillary Clinton"

On June 28, 2010 FBI arrested in New York, Massachusetts, Virginia and New Jersey 10 Russian illegal spies. All were charged as agents of a foreign government ((Russia) and were not registered with the Dept. of Justice , 5 years in jail. Also, all of them except Anna Chapman, were charged with conspiracy to commit money laundering, up to 20 years in jail.

In 2007-2010 Alan Patrikof, a financier, a close friend of Clintons, a sponsor Hillary Clinton's election campaigns, had business contacts with vice president of accounting firm "Morea Financial Services, Inc" (120 Broadway, #1016, New York, NY 20271, 212-608-1080) an SVR illegal Cynthia Murphy ( Lydia Gurieva). So, the whole group was working for Cynthia Murphy who was trying to get access to Hillary Clinton .

Philip J. Crowley, assistant press secretary to the US State Department, made right away the statement:"There is no evidence to suggest that this spy group had U.S. Secretary of State as its principal target".

"Daily News", 09.30.2010 :"One of the accused Russian sleeper spies may have been trying to worm her way into Secretary of State Clinton's circle of high-powered friends. Suspect Cynthia Murphy worked at a downtown financial firm that appears to have put her in contact with Alan Patricof, a New York venture capitalist and top Democratic donor who was a finance chairman of Clinton's 2008 presidential campaign. The federal complaint states that in February 2009, Murphy reported to Moscow that through work, she had met a financier who was "a personal friend" of a current cabinet official and an active political fund-raiser"

On July 9, 2010 they were exchanged for garbage, 4 defectors convicted in Russia. On July 12 Russian leader, PM Vladimir Putin met the group which was official recognition of their merits. On October 10, 2010 , Dmitriy Medvedev, President of Russia , awarded all 10 spies with Russian orders and that means they did a very good job in America destroying its national security.

**Agents Categories:**

A."Garbage" (60%), the "no trust " category.

Recruitment is #1 priority for the officer and a part of his working plan and very often he has to recruit people who are not born agents. You can work with a nice guy, teach him, pay him, press him — and he still avoids any cooperation (busy, sick, on vacation, etc.). It's hard to get rid of him because, first, you have to explain to your superiors why you recruited garbage and second, there's a rule: if you want to be very smart and innovative, a reformer, who came here to start intelligence revolution and get rid of a passive agent, recruit an active one first. Also, agents who work under pressure (blackmail) sooner or later slide into this category.

B. Good agents (30%), middle category. They adhere to the rules of discipline and keep the schedule (that's very important even if there's no information), deliver a lot of information that you have to verify through other sources, but don't show much initiative. Used for regular espionage: go and talk to the object, copy documents, make a recording, take pictures, listen, watch. You can trust them and check often, anyway.

C. Born agents (10%). You are very lucky if you can recruit such people. They betray their country with pleasure and sometimes do not even ask for money because it's in their character — they are looking for adventure or are not happy with their personal or professional life and seek improvement or revenge. They take risks, have good analytical abilities, good education, make (VIP) connections easily, "crack" any object, play the "good guy" whom you can trust. Sometimes they come to you as volunteers, and if they bring valuable stuff — recruit them.

D. Women. Women are a special category here, as elsewhere, and the rule is: if you can't recruit a real agent, you recruit a woman. It's not professional to recruit a woman for a serious operation, but if you want to get to an important object, a woman can introduce you. OK, you can recruit a US Senator's secretary or a typist from the Pentagon, but it will be on your conscience if she gets caught. Such cases entail a life sentence, usually — how would you feel? Besides, women often fall in love with their objects and tell them everything. Finally, a married woman is much bigger problem than a married man.

### Recruitment of a secret source (agent)

Recruit a small number of well-informed people.

Do not recruit:
- psychos
- volunteers (unless it's a "mole" or other government employee who brings you top secret information right away. In a counter-intelligence set-up, a "volunteer" will try to get information about you, telling the minimum about himself)
    - persons with low educational and intellectual level
    - people under 30 or over 70, unless it's a VIP
    - mafia members
    - people who are happy with their lives and careers
The best formula when you recruit is a mix of money and ideology (brainwashing). Recruitment Pyramid

***Priority recruitment candidates in the USA:***
President
The White House staff
The Cabinet and federal agencies
The US Congress
Big corporations
Big scientific institutions
Local politicians
VIP world (celebrities — big media, show biz, big sport)
***Working with à secret sources.***
1. Do not tell the agent about problems and mistakes of the agency, about your personal problems, about other agents, about his own file and compromising information you have on him.
2. Don't show him any classified documents — you might provoke him to sell the information to somebody else.
3. Don't trust your agents too much; they can use you to compromise their personal enemies.
4. Never criticize the source — be an adviser. Don't talk straight if he avoids cooperation or brings you garbage — just reduce or stop payments, or get rid of him.
5. You lose the agent if you don't pay him for a job well done, ask him to "produce" fake information or if you don't care about his

personal security and his personal problems (health, career). And — never give poison to your agent for security reasons.

6.Teach your agent to:

- follow security rules while talking to people, working with the documents and especially meeting the officer (some foreign agencies practice open contacts with many people, hoping that the meeting with the agent won't attract much attention — I don't recommend that)

- always stay calm in stressful situations

- always keep discipline and come in time

- use analytic abilities working with people and documents — ask yourself as many questions as you can

### Checking the source

You can never be sure you are not working with a "double agent," even if he brings you top secret stuff. Besides, agents are human beings and they make mistakes — they forget about security, spend too much money, talk too much and ask extra questions; if arrested they may not play the hero but will tell everything. Anyway, you can check your source:

a. by fake arrest followed by severe interrogation.

b. through provocation (tell him you know about his "double game" and watch his behavior after the meeting (it's good to have a listening device or a camera in his house).

c. by making an analysis of all the information and documents he delivers and comparing it with information from other sources.

d. through other agents.

e. through your "mole" in counter-intelligence (if you're lucky).

f. through technical devices (reading the mail, listening to the phone, secret searching his house and office, watching him through hidden cameras, trying surveillance in the street).

### Agent termination (one-way ticket)

It doesn't happen often but you have to know some special situations when you have to terminate the agent:

1. He knows too much (talks too much) and is ready to betray you.

2. VIP agent (politician) is under suspicion and you can't help him for political reasons (diplomatic, international scandal, etc.) - in such a case an accident could be staged. It happens that the agent is too close to President.

3. Agent was involved in special operations (murders) and is dangerous as a witness.

4. Agent is trying to blackmail you.

5. You need to press (blackmail) other agents.

**Special influence**

*Tortures*

Torture is a category of methods of interrogation designed to shock, hurt and humiliate the object and get information or to make him do something (if used for blackmail). Points to remember:

-ongoing torture decreases pain sensitivity

-people with strong will power take torture as a test

-resistance to torture is often a form of hysterics after arrest

-the object could take himself as a martyr if you torture him too much

-torture could damage object's psyche and you won't be able to work with him (that's why we keep terrorists in Guantanamo Bay without trial – we turn them into idiots)

-people usually trust "after torture information" more than voluntary confessions

-there are different types of torture and professionals often combine them

*Techniques of psychological torture include:*

- fake execution

- complete isolation ("wall therapy")

- daylight deprivation

- forcible narcotics addiction. Here you can use depressants, stimulants, opiates or hallucinogens (psychodelics): depressants (alcohol, barbiturates, anti-anxiety drugs with effects of euphoria, tension reduction, disinhibition, muscle relaxation, drowsiness;

stimulants (cocaine, amphetamine, methamphetamine (crystal meth)

- euphoria, exhilaration, high physical and mental energy, reduced appetite, perceptions of power , and sociability; hallucinogens with effects of euphoria, hallucinations, distorted perceptions and sensations

-making the object observe others being tortured (such as family members)

-abuse of object's national, religious feelings or political views

The effects of psychological torture are: anxiety, depression, fear, psychosis, difficulty concentrating, communication disabilities, insomnia, impaired memory, headaches, hallucinations, sexual disturbances, destruction of self-image, inability to socialize

***Techniques of physical torture include:***

-food, water, sleep deprivation

-damage to vital body organs (brain, lungs, kidneys, liver, private parts) plus electric shock. The brain is particularly dependent on a continuous and stable supply of oxygen and glucose.

-rape

-face deformation

- waterboarding: the object is bound to an inclined board, feet raised and head slightly below the feet. Material is wrapped over the prisoner's face and water is poured over them, asphyxiating the prisoner.

- hypothermia: the object is left to stand naked in a cell kept near 50 degrees Fahrenheit (10 degrees Celsius), while being regularly doused with cold water in order to increase the rate at which heat is lost from the body. A water temperature of 10 °C (50 °F) often leads to death in one hour.

- stress positions: the object is forced to stand, handcuffed and with their feet shackled to an eye bolt in the floor, for more than 40 hours, causing his weight to be placed on just one or two muscles. This creates an intense amount of pressure on the legs, leading first to pain and then muscle failure.

The effects of physical torture are: extreme (unbearable) pain, hypertension, fatigue, cardio-pulmonary and other disorders, brain atrophy.

### Special psychology

1. KGB used "brainwashing" in 4 ways:

a) "prophylactics", which is a conversation/interrogation at KGB field office. After officer gets a "signal" from agent about the 'object", he starts the "file of operative check (DOP)" or "operative development" DOR - means the object is a big enemy). He has 12 months to make a decision what to do to the object – "prophylactics" and behavior modification (followed by possible recruitment) or jail.

b) through agents (objects close friends, neighbors, family members) and "KGB trusted people" (they are not recruited like agents , they are being used for object's profiling). These guys talk to the object, trying to make "positive" influence, get him out of organized anti-government group

c) in a mental clinic where doctors (they are usually KGB trusted people) prove the object that his behavior is not normal, it's anti -social

If all this doesn't work, object will be arrested , convicted and modification will continue -

d) in jail, through assets

### Another strategy - implantation of new ideas in a group.

The process is: isolation from outside world ("information vacuum")—sleep and food limitation (very effective)—"bombing" with slogans - ideological aggression - achieving the result (brain is loaded). The object is now ready to brainwash newcomers.

2. "Behavior modification" (by placing into a group). The process is: initial contact — introduction to a group — mutual interests — mutual activity–mutual ideas — control and prevention of any negative contacts outside the group. No rush, no pressure.

3. Special psychotherapy methods: talk + drugs + blondes +

alcohol (used for recruitment)

*Attention*: An alcoholic is more impulsive, untrustful and unreliable; he demonstrates a poverty of ideas and incapacity for attention. He usually has serious personality maladjustments. He's immature, insecure, oversensitive and anxious. Without alcohol he's unable to meet and enjoy people socially, and suffers from marked feeling of inferiority. Besides, alcoholics suffer from vitamin B1 deficiency, which leads to anatomic changes in the central nervous system and heart with symptoms like anorexia, fatigability, and sleep disturbances. Other common symptoms are irritability, poor memory, inability to concentrate, heart pain.

4. "Transfer" (the object is placed in a regular hospital and then he's transferred to a mental health clinic or jail). In jail you can use such methods an accelerated work schedule (to exhaust the object), turning him into a number to traumatize his psyche, physical punishment or a threat of punishment to keep the object tense and depressed; senseless labor to destroy his personality. Remember: the lower the intellectual level of the object, the more aggressive he is and more sensitive to incentive or punishment.

You can actually re-organize any object's behavior by combining rewards and punishments, exposing him to feared situations and teaching him an instinct of a total (political) obedience.

Punishing the object:

- punishment approach means causing suffering to change the object's behavior
- when object isn't afraid, punishment is less effective
- object might coerced into temporary compliance, that's why he has to be under permanent surveillance after punishment
- present object with choices
- don't threaten, explain the threat and the reward instead
- never lose your patience - in such a way you, behavior modifier, show your power and get respect from
the object

## Technology of Mind Manipulation (MM)

1) Create a steadfast American collective will-power: "We want to live forever in the America we live in now" - through the media.

2) Don't ask people to change their views and beliefs - they have only to change the object of their aggression - "Now we understand who are America's enemies! (the previous President, Republicans).

3) Get people accustomed to accept facts but believe only in the "right" comments - any common sense has to be "switched off." This way you create *"mass artificial schizophrenia"* — people lose the ability to connect statements and facts (notions) and just believe.

Besides, by extreme exaggeration of the enemy's negative qualities you can install *the national schizophrenic fear* (of "international terrorism") and people have to accept you, the US President, as a savior. Plus, no matter what, repeat your major statements until people start accepting them without thinking.

4) Divide the nation into "good Americans"(patriots) and "bad Americans"(the "minority).

Make it clear : it's much better and more comfortable to be "good" than "bad." "We aren't watching good Americans who support the President. The surveillance is for bad Americans and we make their lives and careers uncomfortable. We have to do that because enemies of America may be using them." This method is called artificial social selection and its ultimate goal is a total regulation and standardization of the nation.

5) For successful MM, use the combined efforts of popular Democratic American writers, TV and radio anchors, talented publicists and columnists, business and show business celebrities, politicians. Thus, step by step you create the "industry of correct political behavior and correct American thinking."

6) Use a combination: statement + image. It reduces the effort needed to understand your message and makes people comfortable with you.

7) Shift all popular TV shows to prime time - Americans don't have to think about politics after they come home.

### Blackmail

Used to force a person to do something (or stop the action) against his will; it's used also for recruitment. Blackmail methods include:

1. Leaking "dirt" on the object through media
2. Creating problems in his personal life and career
3. Straight blackmail (threatening to make public certain compromising facts about him)
4. Placing weapons, drugs, secret documents in object's house or office, followed by search and arrest
5. Accusations of rape (robbery) (use hookers for that)
6. Blackmail by pressing family members. Careful, object may commit suicide after intense blackmail, especially if he is an intellectual

### Murders

***Regular***.Shooting, explosives or poison (cyanides, curare). Use a sniper or a "mouse" car (loaded with explosives and parked on the object's route) if access to the object is impossible because of high security. Anyway, the murder is obvious and investigation is inevitable.

General scheme. The best thing to do is to recruit or " install" somebody with access to the object's security system and get information on his schedule (plus health and habits), places where he likes to relax. Get access to his phone and e-mail. Then prepare the plan and train three groups: surveillance (with optics and radios), action (includes snipers, explosives technicians or staged accidents specialists), and security (these people neutralize bodyguards, witnesses and other people who could interrupt the action; they complete the action if the action group fails; and they can neutralize the action group later, if planned so; they "cover" the safe retreat of action group and "cut" the chase).

***Complex***.Staged accidents (suicides, catastrophes, drowning or fall, robbery or rape followed by murder, technical accident (fire, electricity, gas); drugs, weapons, poison, explosives misuse. Staged natural death (stroke, heart attack, chronic illness).

**Strategies.**

Every operation demands a set of original methods, especially if we are talking about strategic intelligence. I give you a few examples.

1. "Domino" or "chain reaction." A coup, revolution or civil war in one country provokes the same actions in other countries (neighbors). It doesn't matter what country is going to be next, most important - what country is a target.

2. "False flag". The planned, but never executed, 1962 Operation Northwoods plot by the U.S. administration for a war with Cuba involved scenarios such as hijacking a passenger plane and blaming it on Cuba.

3. "Sliding" strategy. Transformation of a secret operation into an open one: support of illegal opposition/coup.

4. "Restriction." You damage (limit) international and economic connections (projects) of the enemy.

5. "Monopoly." Special operation to keep country's monopoly or status as economic leader or special (nuclear) holder, or high tech producer. Includes actions to restrict the attempts of other countries to get strategic raw materials and modern weapons and technologies.

6. "Reverse effect." The government declares a certain goal and launches a military or special operation, but the result is something quite different, possibly opposite. Examples: instead of separating (ethnic) group "A" from group "B" both of them are being exterminated; instead of peace and democracy in a certain region, power is being concentrated in one group and the opposition is being exterminated.

7. "Clash." You "clash" the government and opposition of a target country and support civil war until the country is ruined and you get it for free.

8. "Salami-slice strategy". It's a process of threats and alliances used to overcome opposition. It includes the creation of several factions within the opposing political party, and then dismantling

that party from inside, without causing the "sliced" sides to protest.
9. "Positive shock." A domestic operation; to save the government during a crisis, special service provokes artificial civil conflict or sabotage, imitation (terror), and the government takes care of the "problem."

10. "Controlled crisis export" (see "Foreign Policy")

11. "Sanitation border." "Fencing" the target country by enemies (neighbors).

12. "Alibi." You build a "chain" of evidence (witnesses) and move the investigation to a dead end.

13. "Passive sabotage." A very effective strategy used to cover up a major action like the assassination of a President or the destruction of several office towers. You just "do not see the bad guys" who are going to kill the President or blow up the city. In any case you win — the perpetrators are not sure you are watching them; you can arrest them if the object survives or liquidate them once the object is dead. You don't need a big conspiracy, you just give the order to ignore certain people until their plan materializes.

14. "Special tour." You help the target country to "build democratic institutions" (the government and local administrations) by sending official crews to help. Actually, they rule the country and that's a "hidden occupation."

15. "Mask." You mask your actual global plans (reforms) by another big action (war).

16. Illegal espionage operations. Very dangerous , because illegal spy is playing born American and can make career in business, becoming #1 Pentagon supplier or in the government, getting to the Congress or even White House.

17. "Passive sabotage".

On November 22, 1963 , President John Kennedy was assassinated at 12:30 p.m.in Dealey Plaza, Dallas, Texas.

What's conspiracy? It's when you ask the government a simple question and nobody wants to answer it. And if you ask the wrong questions you get the wrong answers, as with the Warren

Commission. Let's ask some good questions.

Question 1. What would have happened if the snipers missed the target or Kennedy survived, being merely wounded- m sniper is a human being - he makes mistakes.

Answer. Kennedy would have won the 1964 Presidential election and then conceivably his brothers, Robert and Edward, would keep the Oval Office until 1984 (count the years for yourself). No war in Vietnam. The CIA would have been shut down. The FBI and Pentagon would have been "cleaned up" and "cleaned out."

Question 2. Why would the CIA, FBI and big business behind them, not to mention others who had their eye on the Oval Office, take such a huge risk?

Answer. There was no risk at all and there was no "huge conspiracy - there was a **"passive sabotage" operation. CIA Director John McCone, FBI Director Edgar Hoover and Secret Service Director James Rowley made a deal not to touch Lee Harvey Oswald until operation is over.**

Question 3. Why was Kennedy murdered in public? President Kennedy was a sick man, taking a lot of pills daily. He had Addison's disease which, in addition to susceptibility to infection can cause weakness, weight loss and low blood pressure; so he was taking cortisone. For his back pain Dr. Max Jacobson injected him (and Jackie) with a mixture of unspecified (!) multivitamins, hormones, steroids, enzymes, and animal organ cells. Kennedy also used cocaine, marijuana, hashish and even LSD, especially during dates with women, including prostitutes —- for many people this was not a secret. There were enough opportunities to stage a death in private.

Answer. This had to be a public execution with a very clear message for the next Presidents - "Don't touch the CIA!" and it worked until now. I want to touch CIA.

Question 4. What was the rush?

Answer. Kennedy wanted to eliminate CIA.

***That's not the end.***

John Kennedy Jr. who said once that his father's death investigation was the most important thing of his life, approached Princess Diana Spencer for an interview for his "George" magazine. They met at New York Carlyle Hotel where JFK dated Marilyn Monroe - a holy place for John Kennedy Jr. where he would never have "hot sex" and "try cocaine" with Diana . It was a business meeting, an "investigation" meeting. In 1995 CIA wanted me to kill somebody very important - it could be Diana and John Kennedy Jr.

August 31, 1997

CIA used my instructions on staged car accidents to kill Princess Diana. Diana was fatally injured in a car crash in the Pont de l'Alma road tunnel in Paris, which also caused the death of her boyfriend, Dodi Fayed.

Billionaire Mohammed al-Fayed, Dodi's father, recruited a "mole" inside CIA, somebody who knew the Agency had a file on Diana. He didn't get it of course through Washington, DC District Court and the mistake was - he had to recruit somebody with straight access to archives. If Diana left a notice on her talks with John Kennedy Jr for her sons, they might be next CIA victims. I can tell Mohammed al-Fayed what's in Diana's CIA file for free - surveillance documents, a video tape of the Carlyle Hotel meeting, a plan to stage the car accident, a file on me if I had to do the job.

If I have to investigate Diana's death, I would start with a very simple question.

What happened to the driver, the Ritz security chief Henri Paul?

He tried to out-run paparazzi by speeding down a Riverfront Expressway, but lost somehow control of the Mercedes S280 near the entrance to the Alma Tunnel and crashed into a concrete pillar at an estimated speed of 65 to 70 miles per hour. He died on impact of a severed spine and a ruptured aorta.

Attention. The tests showed an extraordinary high (not explained until now) level of carbon monoxide in his blood (20.7 %), which should have caused a severe headache, dizziness, confusion and absolute aversion to alcohol. Very heavy smokers can have a level of up to 9% , and Henri Paul wasn't a heavy smoker. There were no ventilation problems in his apartment, office or car. The gas didn't appear from inside Mercedes because no other passanger was affected.

So, what happened to Henri Paul ?

July 16, 1999

CIA killed John Kennedy Jr. in a staged plane crash. Kennedy along with his wife Carolyn and sister-in-law Lauren were reported missing when the Piper Saratoga II HP he was piloting failed to arrive at its planned destination, the Martha's Vineyard Airport in Vineyard Haven, Massachusetts.

A search immediately commenced to locate the trio, ending on July 21 when their bodies were discovered and returned to land. The National Transportation Safety Board (NTSB) determined that the plane had crashed into the Atlantic Ocean off Martha's Vineyard and the probable cause was pilot error: "Kennedy's failure to maintain control of the airplane during a descent over water at night, which was a result of spatial disorientation." Kennedy was not qualified to fly a plane by "instruments only," though the crash occurred in conditions not legally requiring it. Their ashes were scattered from the Navy ship off the coast of Martha's Vineyard.

## SPECIAL STRATEGIES
### Coup d'etat

Coups, like war, are one of the most violent tools of special services and one could be artificially staged in a target country by "feeding" and "pushing" the political opposition or by using VIP agents in the government. Most coups are "Bureaucratic," and entail mainly a change of leader, usually by person #2. That person might be the trigger or might be induced to practice "passive sabotage" and allow certain others to take over. It is also an example of political engineering. Coups usually use the power of the existing government for its own takeover.

Conditions for a successful coup:

-the army is supportive or at least neutral (a coup usually involves control of some active

-portion of the military while neutralizing the remainder of the armed services)

-the leader is out of town (vacation, visit abroad) or is ill

-a political or economic crisis.

-opponents fail to dislodge the plotters, allowing them to consolidate their position, obtain the surrender or acquiescence of the populace, and claim legitimacy

*Military Coup*

Changing a civilian government to a military one, usually in developing countries.

Conditions: a long-term political and economic crisis that threatens national security and the unity of the country. Military chief(s) eventually let the people elect a civilian president and form a civilian government after "re-construction" of political and economic systems. They usually leave for themselves the right to control further political process. A good example is the attempt of anti-Nazi officers to assassinate Hitler in a coup. On July 20, 1944, Colonel Claus Schenk von Stauffenberg brought a bomb-laden suitcase into a briefing room where Hitler was holding a meeting. The bomb exploded and several persons were killed. Hitler was wounded, but his life was saved when the suitcase was unwittingly moved away by someone. Hitler was shielded from the blast by the conference table, leaving him with minor injuries. Subsequently about 5,000 people were arrested by the Gestapo and about 200,including Stauffenberg, were executed in connection with attempt, some on the very same day (which means that Himmler was involved and knew perfectly well about the coup).

*"Democratic" Coup*

A democratic coup would be a change of the government by the most aggressive (nationalistic) political party.
Conditions:
-artificial or actual government crisis
-mass anti-government propaganda
-organized "democratic" movement all over the country
-provoked mass protests (10,000 participants and up) and civil disobedience actions
To provoke a mass anti-government meeting you have to bring to the place well-trained group of agitators (bring as many as you can), and they will inevitably attract an equal number of curious persons who seek adventures and emotions, as well as those unhappy with the government (unemployed people, young and old, are usually very supportive). Arrange transportation of the participants to take them to meeting places in private or public vehicles. Design placards, flags and banners with different radical slogans or key words; prepare flyers, pamphlets (with instructions for the participants), posters and signs (to make the concentration more noticeable). It's good if you place a surveillance team on the top floors of the nearby buildings - they will report any changes in the event; have also messengers to transmit your orders. Remember, if you clash with police and military and a participant(s) is being killed, the conflict inflames right away.

Your people can also infiltrate the spontaneous anti-government meeting and turn it into a mass radical demonstration with fights and incidents. Key agitators (with security attached to them) have to be dispersed and stand by placards, signs, lampposts; they have to avoid places of disturbances, once they have provoked them.
-the leader of the meeting must be protected by a ring of bodyguards (they protect him from police or help him to escape).
-government buildings must be "covered" by a blockade
"Democratic" nationalistic coup in Ukraine (2004), so-called "orange revolution". Scenario: acts of civil disobedience, strikes,

sit-ins (in the central square), aggressive propaganda, mass demands to revote the 2004 Ukrainian presidential election.

Revolution

A change of government and political and economic systems by political gangsters, usually fed, pushed, incited, and possibly funded and equipped by the secret services of another country. Government buildings are blockaded, the government isolated, all communications and transportation systems captured, government media closed, new government formed.
Conditions:
- political and economic crisis
- mass anti-government propaganda (in the army too)
- provoked mass protests and civil disobedience actions
- terror and urban guerillas

**Industrial espionage methods:**

- assets recruitment
- surveillance
- surreptitious entry (including bribery at hotels to allow access to guest and luggage rooms)
- specialized technical operations (communications intelligence and signals intelligence ) and economic disinformation
- using foreign students studying in the USA, foreign employees of US firms and agencies, debriefing foreign visitors to the USA on their return to their home country, recruitment of émigrés, ethnic targeting (suborning or threatening Americans with foreign family ties), and elicitation during international conferences and trade fairs. Agents have also exploited private-sector firms, joint ventures, mergers or acquisitions and non-profit organizations as opportunities and fronts for espionage. Hiring competitors' employees, signing corporate technology agreements, sponsoring research projects in the USA and assigning foreign liaison officers

to government-to-government research and development projects are additional valuable methods for covert data gathering.

- open-source intelligence methods include open or covert use of public databases, hiring information brokers and assigning consultants to gather information for confidential research reports. In some cases foreign interests have paid lobbyists to influence lawmakers and to facilitate extended contacts with high-placed officials with access to valuable information

- bid proposals, energy policies, marketing plans, price structuring, proposed legislation, tax and monetary policies, and control regulations for technology transfer and munitions

- requesting information through e-mail or letters, including apparent responses to advertising or trade show exhibits

# Part 2. COUNTER-ESPIONAGE

**Counter-espionage** refers to efforts made by intelligence organizations, government or corporate, to prevent hostile or enemy intelligence organizations from successfully gathering any classified or confidential information.

### National Counterintelligence Strategy of the United States. 2007

*Why it does not work.*

1."The United States faces substantial challenges to its security, freedom and prosperity. Transnational terrorism, continued proliferation of weapons of mass destruction (WMD),asymmetric warfare, extremist movements, and failed states present severe challenges to a just and stable world".
Wrong. Transnational terrorism does not exist.
2."Subversion, treason and leaks expose our vulnerabilities, our governmental and commercial secrets, and our intelligence sources and methods. This insider threat has been a source of extraordinary damage to U.S. security. Countering this threat will require an aggressive national effort. [We] must develop new methods...For example, electronic systems designed to discover unexplained patterns of activities or anomalous events".
Wrong. New counterespionage methods do not exist. I don't see how "aggressive national effort" could help you find a single "mole".
3."No counterintelligence official can guarantee our nation

will never suffer another incident of treason or espionage. We can, however, assure the President, the Congress, and the American people that we have measurably increased the rigor of our system of national intelligence, and we have put in place systems, practices, and procedures that make foreign penetration more difficult to accomplish and easier to detect".

Wrong. What "systems, practices and procedures"'" are you talking about if Russians pay millions ?

4."We will also provide strategic analysis to the National Security Council".

Wrong. They don't need your strategic analysis. They need the "moles" names .

5."The armed forces' effectiveness depends on their ability to conduct military operations uncompromised by adversaries' foreknowledge. The obligation to support such operations extends beyond the Defense Department to the entire counterintelligence community".

Wrong. Exchange of classified infortmation within government agencies is a huge problem, because it's all about security of secret sources. I'm absolutely against this practice.

6."The increasing complexity of counterintelligence challenges…"

Wrong. They are the same for the last one hundred years.

**Gestapo : what I recommend**

1."Public places total control" method: assets were recruited at every big restaurant, bar, hotel or store. They delivered information on any client whose behavior was somewhat different from the general one: too excited or too depressed, too greedy or too generous, too open or too "closed", etc. And very often such a client deserved special attention.

2.Aggressive total recruitment — by the end of World War II

there wasn't a single guerilla detachment, resistance or espionage group on occupied Soviet and European territories that had not been in part or completely eliminated by the GESTAPO or SD — 100 per cent professional counter-terrorist and counter-espionage job based on infiltration.

3. The "Night and Fog" operation. By 1941 the Gestapo analysts reported that the "taking hostages" practice was not effective any more as resistance on the occupied territories was even increasing after that went into effect. Instead, resistance fighters had to be secretly arrested and transported to Germany where, after investigation, they just vanished without a trace.

4. "Third degree" interrogation.

### "Moles"

A "mole" is a spy inside the government, recruited or "installed" most often within the special services, by an outside government/agency. The 3 most dangerous things a "mole" can do:

1. Calculate President's plans and decisions judging by information he's asking for.

2. Manipulate information being sent to President, and thus influence global political decisions .

3. Paralyze to some extent the government (if he's CIA or FBI Director)

#### *Methods to detect a "mole"*

A. Index cards (special file) — never use computers to save this information!

Prepare a file on each officer and mark there the signs of a "mole" — has or spends too much money, asks too many extra questions; uses professional skills to check for physical and technical surveillance; has discreet contacts with foreigners; discreet copying of top secret documents; attempts to get a job in most secret departments; talks with close friends and family members about the possibility of making money as a "mole"; behavior deviations — extra suspiciousness, excitement, depression, drugs or alcohol addiction. Three signs are enough to start an investigation — the "triangulation" principle.

B. Use provocation. If a prospective "mole" is looking for a contact with the enemy and is ready to betray, and you have exact information, organize such a "meeting" for him. Do not arrest the person right away — play along, as he may give you connections to other people who are ready to betray. There's one more provocation method: you supply the suspects with "highly classified information" and just watch what they do.

C. Use "filter" or "narrowing the circle." Include all the officers you suspect in a "circle" and narrow it until one name is left as the most likely suspect.

D. Make a "model" of a "mole," judging by information you have on him.

E. Recruit an insider. Recruit a "mole" inside your enemy's intelligence service and he'll help you to find the one inside yours (it's called "grabbing the other end of a thread").

F. "Triangulation" (see above).

*What to do if you detect a "mole"*

- assess the damage

- restrict his access to classified information and start "feeding" him with fake data

- stop all operations he was involved in and create the illusion they are still in progress

- bring home officers and agents who work abroad and had contacts with him and those to whose files he had access

- start 24/7 surveillance if you've decided to play the game and look into his contacts

- arrest the "mole" discreetly (if you want to continue the game)

How to Cover Your "Mole"

There are special methods to cover your own "mole" and a "switch" is the most effective — it's when you "switch" counterintelligence to other, innocent persons who work with the "mole." You can try information "leaks" through a "double agent" — it looks like you receive top secret information through another traitor or by breaking the electronic security systems. Or you can try information "leak" through publications in big newspapers — it looks like information is not secret and is known to many people or there's another "mole."

### *Identifying Spies*

If a spy is an intelligence officer working abroad under "cover" (diplomat, businessman, reporter) you can identify him by:

- following the careers of all diplomats who work at your enemy's embassies all over the world
- recruiting a "mole" inside the intelligence service (or inside the station)
- setting up your agent for recruitment by the enemy's station
- watching foreigners who try to make discreet contacts with native citizens with access to secrets
- making a model of a spy (professional behavior, attempts to detect surveillance, attempts to recruit sources or just get any classified information during normal meetings, "throwing away" money trying to get access to government employees, military and scientific circles)
- using secret surveillance and listening devices inside the station and practicing secret searches

If a spy is an intelligence officer working in your country under "cover" of a native citizen (or he is recruited by a native citizen) you identify him by making a model (contacts with identified spies — that's often the only sign which points out a spy, and that's why surveillance is very important in getting information **from a "mole"**).

### John Deutch case

Deutch was born in Belgium to a Russian father and he was the only Russian CIA Director. He got some jobs with top secrets access positions :

1977-1980 The US Department of Energy: Director of Energy Research

Acting Assistant Secretary for Energy Technology
Under Secretary
1980-1981 President's Nuclear Safety Oversight Commission
1983 President's Commission on Strategic Forces
1985-1989 The White House Science Council
1990-1993 The President's Intelligence Advisory Board
1993-1994 Under Secretary of Defense for Acquisition and Technology
Deputy Defense Secretary
1995-1996 Director of Central Intelligence
1996 The President's Commission on Aviation Safety and Security
1998-1999 Chairman of the Commission to Assess the Organization of the Federal Government to Combat the Proliferation of Weapons of Mass Destruction

He was appointed by President Clinton and stayed in Langley in 1995-1996. He ordered my recruitment , he is a Russian "mole," and he's safe because Bill Clinton obstructed the investigation and pardoned this enemy of state in 2001.

**3 signs are enough to triangulate a "mole" and here they are for Mr. Deutch:**
1. Two days after Deutch retired from the CIA, on December 16, 1996, technical personnel discovered at his house highly classified information stored on his unclassified computer, loaded from his agency computer. He refused to explain why he violated strict security rules.

First, Director of Central Intelligence doesn't need highly classified data on his home computer, because he is a bureaucrat, not an analyst.

Second, here we have a trick - the Internet-connected computer is accessible by anyone with some technical knowledge and you don't have to send anything — Russians will read secret information right from your home computer.

2. In 1997 the CIA began a formal security investigation. It was

determined that his computer was often connected to Internet with no security, and that Deutch was known to leave memory cards with classified data lying in his car. Deutch used his influence to stop further investigation and the CIA took no action until 1999, when it suspended his security clearances. He admitted finally the security breach and merely apologized but refused to explain communication via Internet with some Russian chemist.

3. In 1999 the Defense Department started its own investigation, and it appeared that in 1993 Deutch, as Defense Undersecretary, used unsecured computers at home and his America Online (!) account to access classified defense information. As Deputy Defense Secretary, he declined departmental requests in 1994 to allow security systems to be installed in his residence.

4. In 2000 Senator Charles Grassley asked the Justice Department to look into the case. There was no investigation

In 2001 President Clinton, KGB secret source, pardoned Deutch. There were no comments.

Since 2000 Deutch is MIT Professor and Director for Citigroup. Very good.

### The most stupid "mole" in the history of espionage

1984. KGB major Sergey Motorin,very smart guy, who worked at KGB station in Washington, DC , decided to buy TV+video set for $950 at one of the stores. He asked for a discount and the owner, FBI source, told him they could make a deal - Motorin could pay half of the money with Russian vodka "Stoli".

Motorin bought at the Soviet Embassy two boxes ( $4.50 a bottle) and came next day to the store. FBI agents were already waiting for him - they blackmailed and recruited Motorin.

In 1985 walk-in recruit , CIA agent Ames Aldrich, gave KGB the name of the traitor.

Motorin was called back to Moscow "for a new assignment", arrested at the airport, convicted and executed.

**Special tools**

Surveillance

Actual espionage is not what you see in the movies and you have absolutely no chance of evasion if a real professional surveillance crew is following you. Why? Because they use multiple methods and mixed methods.

Physical surveillance.

*Methods*

1. "One line" - officers follow the object forming a line behind him and passing him one by one.
2. "Two lines" - officers form two lines on both sides of the street.
3. "Circle" - officers block the area and start searching (used in case they lose the object).
4. "Fork" - one officer (a car) moves in front of the object, another one — behind, other officers (cars) move along parallel streets.
5. "Box" - used when the object enters supermarket, hotel, restaurant. One or two officers follow the object, the others wait for him at the exits.
6. "Demonstration" - officers demonstrate their presence to press the object and lower his activity.
7. "Provocation" - officers attack the object, beat him, steal (secret) documents. Often used to lower his activity if he's trying to play James Bond.
8. "Outstrip" - officers do not follow the object because they know exactly where he's going.
9. "Football" - officers pass the object to each other (car — a group — bicyclist — car...)
10. "Movie" - the crew watches the object in stages: first day — to the subway only, second day — from subway to his office,

etc. (used abroad). The crew has to have a female member if they are watching a woman (she could use the ladies room for a secret meeting) and members of various ethnicities (white, black, Latino) because the object could go to a specific ethnic area.

**If you're the object and you've noticed surveillance**
Don't rush, move at the same speed.

Relax at the nearest bar (and relax the crew).

Don't show how professional you are by trying to disappear, otherwise they could intensify surveillance or even neutralize you (smash your car, beat you up).

Postpone the operation you were engaged in .

Use a "draught" if you need to see your agent no matter what. Change lanes (if you are driving), stop the car and then drive left or right.

If you don't see surveillance, that means either there's no surveillance or you've failed in counter-surveillance. Discreetly watch the agent who's coming to meet you and try to detect any possible surveillance; or you may have been "outstripped."

**Surveillance crew mistakes**
The same crew follows the object all day long.

The object "rules" the crew and calculates it (he moves faster — the crew moves faster).

A crew member is too noticeable (unusual dress, haircut, disabled parts of the body, too fat or too skinny, too ugly or too pretty).

The crew starts to search possible hiding places for espionage evidence right after the object leaves (and he may be watching).

The crew leaves traces after a secret search of the object's house (office).

The crew does not report its mistakes or the fact that they've lost the object.

The crew is not professional (using childish tricks like jumping out of a subway train just before the doors close).

### Technical Surveillance

1. Visual surveillance. Done through special holes in the ceilings and walls, through the windows from the opposite building (car) or by installing the camera inside the house (you can substitute something, like a clock, for the same thing but "stuffed" with a camera or recorder.) You can use informant as well to watch the object outside his house (especially if you want to do a secret search).

2. Listening devices. The easiest thing is to listen to the object's phone (record all calls, including those dialed "by mistake"). If you work inside his apartment, make sure you equip the room where he usually talks. Attention: avoid widespread mistake when your agent keeps the listening device on his body; install a miniature device in his clothes or shoes, because the object could try a test and ask the agent to take off his clothes or invite him to the sauna or pool.

3. If you are working abroad, listen 24/7 to local counterintelligence surveillance radiofrequencies.

4. Reading the mail. When you control the object's mail, remember he could use multiple addresses and PO boxes. Open all the letters with no return address or PO box. Watch when you open the letter — the object could leave a tiny piece of paper, hair, etc. to check if anybody opened the letter. Analyze the text carefully — there could be a cipher or the words with double meaning (jargon), especially when you read mafia mail.

5. Combination of above-mentioned methods

### *Interrogation*

Interrogation is a conversational process of information gathering. The intent of interrogation is to control an individual so that he will either willingly supply the requested information or, if someone is an unwilling participant in the process, to make the person submit to the demands for information.

Remember, people tend to:

-talk when they are under stress and respond to kindness and understanding.

-show deference when confronted by superior authority, This is culturally dependent, but in most areas of the world people are used to responding to questions from a variety of government and quasi-government officials.

-operate within a framework of personal and culturally derived values. People tend to respond positively to individuals who display the same value system and negatively when their core values are challenged.

-respond to physical and, more importantly, emotional self-interest.

-fail to apply or remember lessons they may have been taught regarding security if confronted with a disorganized or strange situation

-be more willing to discuss a topic about which the interrogator demonstrates identical or related experience or knowledge

-appreciate flattery and exoneration from guilt

Procedure

Before you interrogate the object, you have to gather some intelligence on him — examine his documents, read his files (if any), interrogate his partners or co-workers. Then you must establish and develop rapport, when the object reacts to your statements. Rapport may be developed by asking background questions about his family, friends, likes, dislikes; by offering incentives like coffee, alcohol, cigarettes, meals, or offers to send a letter home; by feigning experiences similar to those of the object; by showing concern for the object through the use of voice vitality and body language; by helping the source rationalize his guilt; by flattering the object. Be convincing and sincere, and you'll control the object for sure.

After that you can start questioning using follow-up questions (they flow one from another based on the answer to previous questions), break-up questions (to "break" the object's concentration, if he's lying, by interrupting him all the time), repeated questions (to check the previous information), control questions (developed from information you believe to be true and based on information which has been recently confirmed and which is not likely to be changed. They are used to check the truthfulness of the object's responses and should be mixed in with other questions throughout the interrogation), prepared questions developed in advance of interrogation to gain precise wording or the most desirable questioning sequence (they are used primarily for interrogations which are technical in nature), leading questions (to prompt the object to answer with the response he believes you wish to hear) to verify information.

There are two types of questions that you should not use - these are compound and negative questions. Compound questions are questions which ask for at least two different pieces of information and they are, actually, two or more questions in one. They allow the object to avoid giving a complete answer. Negative questions are questions which are constructed with "no," "not," "none." They should be avoided because they may confuse the object and produce false information.

Never allow the suspect to deny guilt. But it's good if he is involved in discussion and gives you the reason why he didn't or couldn't commit the crime, because you can prove he's wrong and move him towards offering alternatives and giving two choices for what happened; one more socially acceptable than other. The suspect is expected to choose the easier option but whichever alternative he chooses, guilt is admitted. Also, offer punishment alternatives and deals and lead the suspect to repeat the admission of guilt in front of witnesses.

*Tricks:*

a) "good cop / bad cop"
b)"story under a story" (after intense interrogation the object

tells a different story — which is not true, either)
c) "bombing" with questions
d) pressure by not interrogating
e) "silence makes your situation worse" trick
f) "admit one small episode and that's it" trick
g) "I help you — you help me" trick
h) "shift" - try to shift the blame away from the suspect to some other person or set of circumstances that prompted the subject to commit the crime. That is, develop themes containing reasons that will justify or excuse the crime. Themes may be developed or changed to find one to which the accused is most responsive.

Remember, every object has a breaking point and there are some indicators that the object is near his breaking point or has already reached it. If the object leans forward and his facial expression indicates an interest in the proposal or is more hesitant in his argument, he is probably nearing the breaking point.

**If you are being interrogated**, your major objective is to buy time and use "effective talking," disclosing information that is correct, but outdated or worthless. I can add also a few words about the polygraph ("lie detector") , which measures heart rate, blood pressure, respiration rate, and skin conductivity to detect emotional arousal, which in turn supposedly reflects lying versus truthfulness. The polygraph does in fact measure sympathetic nervous system arousal, but scientific research shows that lying is only loosely related to anxiety and guilt. Some people become nervous when telling the truth, whereas others remain calm when deliberately lying. Actually, a polygraph cannot tell which emotion is being felt (nervousness, excitement, sexual arousal) or whether a response is due to emotional arousal or something else, such as physical exercise. Although proponents contend that polygraph tests are 90% or more accurate, tests show error rates ranging between 25 and 75 percent. My own experience says that you can successfully lie to polygraph. In 1987, while at KGB Andropov Intelligence

Institute, I was tested by "lie detector", and I failed the first set of questions, like :" Have you ever cheated on your wife?" or "Do you like prostitutes?". Then I relaxed for half an hour watching other students going through the procedure, and took the test again – this time I tried to stay absolutely indifferent and "programmed" to lie. I won . I think, the best thing is to use "guilty knowledge" questions to make the polygraph reliable – that is, questions based on specific information that only a guilty person would know ( such as the place where the object (a "mole") had a "brush contact" with intelligence officer) – the idea is that guilty person would recognize these specific cues and respond in a different way than an innocent person. action officer - the case officer designated to perform an operational act during a clandestine operation, especially in hostile territory.

### REID TECHNIQUE
**Through my experience**

1. One goal of interrogation, therefore, is to reduce perceived consequences of telling the truth. Legally, an investigator cannot reduce real consequences (offer a promise of leniency in exchange for a confession).

Wrong. I can reduce real consequences if I'm interested in the object - he has good connections and I want to recruit him. I don't pay attention to some details and the evidence which might send him to jail for a long time. Even if he goes to jail, it's much better for him to go there as KGB asset.

2. Consequently, one technique that should be avoided is to inform the suspect about the possible sentence facing him if he is convicted. The investigator who tells a suspect, "You're in a lot of trouble and face the next 20 years behind bars," has made it psychologically very difficult for the suspect to tell the truth.

Wrong. The first question "moles" ask is :"How many years I'll get ? They might execute me ?" You can tell him the truth but don't put all the cards on the table (evidence).

3. Another technique to reduce perceived consequences of a crime involves more active persuasion. In this instance, the suspect is told that his crime could have been much worse and that it is fortunate that the suspect did not engage in the more serious activity.
Right.
4. The second principle is that every person who has committed a crime will have justified the crime in some way. A crime against a person is often justified by blaming the victim (the rape victim encouraged the sexual encounter; the robbery victim was showing off his wealth; or the murder victim got the suspect angry).Related to this principle is a concept termed forming a "victim mentality." Criminals believe that they are the casualty of an unjust and unfair criminal justice system.
Right. "Moles" usually say that they wanted to get as much intel as possible about the enemy (USA gov) and then bring the stuff to KGB.

The Reid Nine Steps of Interrogation
1.The direct positive confrontation. Advise the suspect that the investigation clearly indicates that he is responsible for the commission of a crime.
Right.
2. Theme development. Offer moral or psychological excuses for the suspect's criminal behavior.
Wrong. The suspect has to offer excuses himself and you have to either except them or not.
3-4. Statements the suspect makes during theme development. Most guilty suspects and all innocent ones will offer denials during theme development.
Wrong. You have to close the "gate" completely at the beginning of interrogation - no denial. That's very important - he can't say "I didn't do it".
5. To procure the suspect's attention to the theme. At this stage the investigator may move his chair in closer to the suspect's. A person who is physically close to another individual is also emotionally

closer to that person. The investigator may also ask hypothetical questions designed to stimulate internal thoughts from the suspect. For the first time during the interrogation, the suspect may begin to think about telling the truth. This is termed being in a "passive mood." The behavioral signs at this stage of an interrogation include dropped barriers (uncrossing arms or legs), a less tense posture, eye contact focused to the floor and sometimes tears.

Right.

6. Responding to the suspect's passive mood . The investigator condenses theme concepts to one or two central elements and moves into the next step of the process designed to elicit the initial admission of guilt.

Right.

7. Presenting an alternative question. Examples of an alternative question include, "Have you done this many times before or was this just the first time?" "Was this whole thing your idea or did you get talked into it?"

Right.

8. Developing the oral confession.

Right.

9. The oral confession is converted to a court admissible document. A confession is a statement acknowledging personal responsibility for a crime including details only the guilty person would know.

Right.

**INTERVIEW WITH NEUROLAW PRACTITIONER, November 12, 2011**

1. Under the "Spy Code", #1 is 'no mercy, no ideology and no emotions'. Do they do any type of behavioral deviation training, do you learn as you go, or do they look for these qualities in candidates for KGB?

Answer.

No mercy, no emotions - that's training. You sit on a chair, a gun shot, they kick they chair, you fall on the floor, they check blood pressure and pulse - must be close to normal.

No ideology - that's experience. You don't have to think about Christian religion or Communist Code "A man to a man is a friend and brother" when you kill a man you never saw before and who did nothing wrong to you. You have the order - do the job.

2. What happens when a person would want to leave KGB? What was the most satisfying thing about being a KGB agent?

Answer.

Agent is KGB secret source or asset, let's stick to it. If you talk about KGB officer, call him officer or operative.

If he's counterespionage agent working in Russia, it's not a big problem, though he has to explain the reason.

If he's espionage agent, "mole", the KGB decision depends on how much he knows ( if it's gonna be international scandal if he goes to FBI).

In some cases he might get "one way ticket" (politician, White House, Congress)

3. "Lonely people live longer in espionage business." Why is that do you think? Is it impossible to have it all? Were you able to keep close with your family? Or was there a distance at all times?

Answer.

DO NOT TRUST A WOMAN. Only your mother.

4. Does this tie in with the KGB humor of 'never make friends inside the KGB'? Why is that?

The thing is , KGB has a very strong inner security service. And if they ask you to report on your closest friend - you'll do it without thinking, because your friend might be a traitor.

5. Were many people rejected from KGB?

Answer.

You mean, walk-ins ? Yes, there are psychos and people playing games , pretending they know something and thinking Russians are idiots.

6. Did you work alone or with a crew mostly? How does sniper work fit in?

"Kremlin" operation I was working alone.

Sniper goes into 4 categories:

a) military sniper - he works with a partner, who's looking for the targets using optics

Woman are the best snipers (they usually have lower blood pressure than man and they pay more attention to details. In Chechnya, Russian small Muslim republic where terrorists fight for independence since 1993, they pay women -snipers(soldiers of fortune) from former Soviet Baltic republics(Litva, Estonia) to fight Russian army. Every woman has 2 helpers - they count the dead bodies and keep an eye on the sniper.

b) mafia snipers - work mostly as a team

c) espionage government agency snipers - might be a solo, might be a team, depends

d) "lonely wolves" - psychos who just shoot people in the street through a hole in a van, from the roof, etc.

I prefer to work alone.

7. It seems women as agents were frowned upon, they were seen as a liability due to emotional weakness? Trust issues with them?

Answer.

Absolutely.

8. What would you say the percentage of female agents in the KGB was?

I had altogether around 100 agents, 5 women. There's one very sensitive point with women agents - when they transfer the officer to other office, other city, he has to introduce the agents to his successor. I had 3 cases when women refused to work with other officers.

9. Are there many KGB still in operation now, where are they, what is their general mission and who do they work for?
Answer.
Good question.
First, KGB isn't gone with USSR collapse. Russia saved KGB methods 100% because Putin is a former KGB, as you know. Russia separated counterespionage agency (FSB) from espionage (SVR) but it's all KGB, supporting Putin as a dictator. Nothing changed.
Second, former KGB officers get pension and work mostly in security business if they want. Many of them are agents.

10. Can you elaborate on the" triangulation" principle? Are there any other main principles?
"Triangulation" is just the beginning and it doesn't actually matter that the object is a traitor but it's enough to start the "Espionage" file on him.
Main principle is a TOTAL SECRECY especially if the object is a professional intelligence officer. One small wrong question from the agent and he will understand everything and stop his activity forever or disappear.

11. Where was most of your work focused? What was your specialty?
Answer.
KGB Counterintelligence field office, then KGB Espionage Division, "American direction", with American citizens. Then SBU espionage against Russia.

12. Why don't effective methods to prevent treason exist?
Answer.
Why Americans betray their country,
a).There's no nation. 10 years ago American sociologists admitted that it's no more a "melting pot", it's a "multi-pieces blanket".
I agree. America is a set of closed communities which do not

communicate between each other and don't care about each other. Say, Chinese, Italian and Orthodox Jews – is this one nation ? No way.

b). Money is everything. Ego is everything. American dream is a triangle which doesn't include patriotism:
- 1,000,000 in the bank
- private house
- good education for kids

The story of Aldrich Ames is a good example. Ames was assigned to the CIA's Europe Division/Counterintelligence branch, where he was responsible for directing the analysis of KGB intelligence operations. The information Ames provided led to the execution of at least 10 U.S. secret sources, mostly KGB officers. KGB paid Ames $4.6 million, and with that money he bought a new $60,000 Jaguar (that was his official salary ), jewelry, designer clothing and a house in Northern Virginia valued $500,000 and paid in cash. In 1986 and in 1991, Ames passed two polygraph screening examinations. Ames and his wife liquidated about $2.5 million of the KGB money (they still have $2.1 million in a Russian bank account).

How he was recruited ? He brought 3 names of Washington , DC KGB station officers and asked 50,000. He said that the one-time deal, he won't be back. But Russians said that they would pay him $50,000 each time he wanted to see them, no matter what information he had. Ames agreed right away.

13. What is the most difficult thing to do in espionage?
To recruit somebody who doesn't care about money. To recruit a woman you love. To recruit a son or daughter and ask them to work against their family members. To kill.

14. You mentioned when you first started you were "paid as a traitor", what does that mean? why was that done?
Answer.
Agents get their fee. When I was KGB agent in 70's it was $30-

$40 a month which was OK (regular salary in Soviet Union was $100-$150).

15. What was the most satisfying job you did? What was the worst, and why?
Answer.
Satisfying - when I started getting into Russian big politics as SBU spy. Very satisfying - when I wrote "The Professional" for Bill Clinton.

16. Did you feel any stress of constant "acting" or was it very natural to you?
Answer.
It's a job. If you take it as 'acting" you are not a born spy.

17. What is the most dangerous aspect to avoid pertaining to national security?
Answer.
Underestimate Russians and Chinese.

18. When was the first time you first stopped believing in Communism as a viable system for societal success? or is it still viable in some way you think?
Answer.
I never believed in Communism. The thing is - KGB officers were 100% Communists but KGB was very independent, it was a "state inside a state". Communism is dead end project because if there's no competition, there's no quality and there's no progress.

19. What has 30 years in this field taught you about people? society? and power?
Answer.
Nothing new. A human being wants 2 things: to get pleasure and avoid pain.

20. Did you have any beliefs or illusions that were shattered along the way?
Answer.
I believed that in America they pay you what you deserve.

21. What do you see as your main purpose moving forward?
Answer.
America has no national security system.

22. In doing over 30 interrogations, what was the most effective method you found in getting reliable, accurate information?
Answer.
"Breaking" method.

The most important thing is to make the "object" talk by telling him that you want to just to understand what happened and we , together, may find the way to deal somehow with the situation which "is not very bad right now". The "object", of course, will lie to you , but it doesn't matter - he's talking ,he "swallowed the bait". You listen to him , you write down everything and then you break his story into episodes. Then you start interrogating him on each episode but in chaotic order, like episode #1, then #5, then #the last one, #4, etc. It's pretty hard for the object keep logical lying if you act like this - he'll change his story and put some true details to make it real. Extract those details and help him to tell the truth around them.

23. If several methods were used, are they used in a specific order (i.e. the order in which you listed them on the email you sent me?) Or was it dependant on the object's demeanor/personality or urgency of obtaining the info?
Answer.
Let me tell you most important thing about tortures.
If you deal with a "lonely wolf" (self-made terrorist) who won't talk, you have no choice but to torture him to get info on his possible connections, place where he's keeping guns or explosives, etc.

But if you interrogate a member of organization, you MUST HAVE ASSETS INSIDE THIS ORGANIZATION and you don't have to torture anybody.

National security isn't CIA and FBI #1 priority , that's why they mostly wait for walk-in recruits (I call it a "Newton syndrom" or "falling apple" principle).

You, probably, read the books or watched movies where Gestapo arrested the whole resistence group, tortured the heroes, then hanged them. Why should Gestapo torture the "heroes" if the asset gave them everything ?

24. How often would the interrogation warrant moving to torture type procedures, please give a % if necessary.

Answer.

It's impossible to determine, it depends how professional you are, how you use methods and tricks, how fast you can establish rapport.

25. American detectives using the Reid technique have a significant problem eliciting false confessions from accused offenders using minimization and maximization tricks; in your experience has any unreliable/untrue info ever elicited from interrogation? How about torture? What do you attribute that to?

Answer.

The thing is, if you deal with a professional, he usually has "a story under the story" which he offers you as true after intensive interrogation and tortures (people tend to believe info they get after torturing the object). But he can't lie to me if I have enough intel on , say, his organization . That's very important - how well are you prepared for interrogation.

26. When you detect that the object's will has broken in an interrogation, what is the first question you ask?

Answer.

Nothing. Do not rush the object, do not humiliate him to show you're ,finally, a winner and he's the loser - he's gonna close up. Just keep on developing the talk, don't jump out of your chair, be quiet. It's like a poker.

27. Did using torture procedures always pay off in some way, or was the object destroyed in the process? How often?
Answer.
I made conclusion in 10 minutes whether the guy gonna talk if tortured - body language, face expression, voice, reaction to the tricks, reaction to the facts I have. Torture is like war - you can't win, you start shooting.

28.How did you confirm the info they provided was true, before moving on it?
Answer.
It depends if you have other sources, other facts, documents and how fast you can check up the information.

29. Have there ever been major plans or decisions made around information obtained from torture that was later found be incorrect?
Answer:
Of course. If a radical Muslim fanatic gives you something it's a 100% fake - make whatever decisions you want.

On the other side, war demands fast and true confessions. Sabotage and intelligence unit brings two enemy officers - they have choice: the one who talks first, stays alive.

30.Is the FSB is now more powerful than the KGB was in Soviet times?
Answer.
Yes, funding is much more better and because Putin, Russia's leader, is a former KGB.

31.Explain, in your opinion of the roles/relations of CIA, FBI and former KGB.

Answer.

No relations. KGB was recruiting "moles" inside CIA and FBI, they were doing the same inside KGB. Right now FBI is allowed to have their own espionage stations abroad and recruit foreigners (like CIA).

32. What did you never expect to learn/experience?
Answer.
You can buy anybody, everything has a price.

33. What personality qualities besides 'no emotion, guarded trust' is best to have?
Answer.
a) sense of humor (towards yourself too)
b) talent to listen - for a spy that's a law

34. What is the biggest misconception about KGB?
Answer.
KGB has the right to decide whom to kill.

35. What does the world have right about KGB?
Answer.
The best national security agency in the world.

36. Most psych studies re: interrogation techniques confirm coercion/torture don't elicit reliable info. Since they worked for you and other associates in the field, do you consider these results to be only applicable in the lab?
Answer.
You know, my first interrogation was a disaster. I didn't go to the library, I asked my boss for help. He interrogated hundreds and he cracked my object in 10 minutes. Experience.

37. How were eyewitness reports (decades worth of research showing the unreliability of eyewitness testimony) treated? With

100%confidence?

Answer.

Eyewitness reports serve the general picture. Pictures, DNA samples, fingerprints - they are crime solvers.

### 38. Torture: what about genital mutilation?

Answer.

It all depends on the situation. If it's war and intel/sabotage team got the enemy officer, they have to get intel from him fast and kill him after that. Again, if you got a terrorist with a bomb , and you have no idea who he is and whether his partners a mile away are preparing to blow up Empire State Building tomorrow morning, you have to torture. But if it's Al Qaida guy and you torture him because you have no sources inside major terror organization, you better find another job. You are not professional, you are a garbage.

### 39. Did it ever go to far? Killing the object before info was obtained?

Answer.

You can't kill the object before – why should you ? It's different if you have three terrorists and you torture and kill one of them in front of others just to show what you gonna do to them. Often people take "light" death' as a reward.

### 40. What happened to them after an interrogation? Prison?

Answer.

Again, it depends what you have. If it's an enemy of state and he was involved in serious stuff like coup-d-etat, murders, etc, it's prison. But if you recruit him during interrogation (it happens sometimes) his life in prison will be different. Then, if it's a minor stuff, like talking about the possibility to, say, kill the President, the guy has to sign the paper, promise he won't do it again and he's free . Of course, in this particular case he'll be under surveillance and surrounded by assets for life.

41. Can you tell me about any interrogations you were involved in?

Answer.

The objects were mostly enemies of state, anti-Soviets, anti-Communists, radical nationalists. You can interrogate them only if you have strong evidence. But they are mostly intelligent people and in the cell they might be pressed by my assets – beaten up, raped – "Get the money or we gonna do this every night!" After that interrogation is much easier.

42. How about any torture session that stands out?

Answer.

There's a good and simple one – put pens between your left hand fingers and squeeze them with you right hand . How you feel ?

43. Just to clarify: regarding "keeping the terrorists in Guantanamo Bay without trial – we turn them into idiots" Are you saying the torture used to against them to gain information deteriorates their competency to stand trail?

Answer.

100 %

44. "People usually trust "after torture information" more than voluntary confessions". Why is that when they have been shown in research to be false and in other scenarios to gain false info to make the torture stop?

Answer.

Because that's natural – you expect the enemy to lie to you because he's the actual enemy.

45. How many of your objects responded to torture and gave correct info?

Answer.

I never tortured people. I never interrogated the object without strong evidence and there was no need to torture.

46. Most effective method of torture?
Answer.
You can tell that a certain method was effective if the information was the truth. Say, the guy after torture said "2345 23rd Ave is the terrorists warehouse", you came there, you ambushed the place and got the terrorists – the method was effective.

47. How was interrogating "moles" or other highly trained officials who were trained as you were and knew what to expect?
Answer.
Extremely difficult. You must have a very, very strong case.

48. I like the idea of comparing/contrasting your experience with interrogation with the Reid technique used here in the U.S. I then will add study findings to the mix. To make this more dynamic.... could you add comments to the ones that were" RIGHT" ..for example - why is that right.... how do you know it's right.....any pointers on how to ensure its done correctly ..... indicators...why it is important...anecdotal info.....I think this is interesting since there are so many commonalities, and people still have a notion that KGB would be harsher, less rules, more freedom to destroy object--when in fact many of the guidelines/pointers are the same.
Answer.
REID 1. One goal of interrogation, therefore, is to reduce perceived consequences of telling the truth. Legally, an investigator cannot reduce real consequences (offer a promise of leniency in exchange for a confession).
Wrong. I can reduce real consequences if I'm interested in the object - he has good connections and I want to recruit him. I don't pay attention to some details and the evidence which might send him to jail for a long time. Even if he goes to jail, it's much better for him to go there as KGB asset.
REID 2. Consequently, one technique that should be avoided is to inform the suspect about the possible sentence facing him if he is convicted. The investigator who tells a suspect, "You're in a

lot of trouble and face the next 20 years behind bars," has made it psychologically very difficult for the suspect to tell the truth.

Wrong. The first question moles ask is: "How many years I'll get? They might execute me?" You can tell him the truth but don't put all the cards on the table (evidence).

REID 3. Another technique to reduce perceived consequences of a crime involves more active persuasion. In this instance, the suspect is told that his crime could have been much worse and that it is fortunate that the suspect did not engage in the more serious activity.
Right. Minimize the situation? Why is this good?

Because it makes him talk, you encourage the enemy of state to tell the truth, lying to him that for his crime, say , participation in a terror group, he might not even go to jail. "Other bastards brainwashed you, blackmailed you, threatened you, broke your will power - they will go to jail for sure. And you - you were forced to make a wrong decisions. now it's time to make a right decision and tell the truth about bastards who wanted to ruin your life".
On top of it you can add a trick:" And you know what ? They talk right now and they set you up saying you were the leader of the group, you pushed them to blow the bombs, understand ?"

REID 4. The second principle is that every person who has committed a crime will have justified the crime in some way. A crime against a person is often justified by blaming the victim (the rape victim encouraged the sexual encounter; the robbery victim was showing off his wealth; or the murder victim got the suspect angry).Related to this principle is a concept termed forming a "victim mentality." Criminals believe that they are the casualty of an unjust and unfair criminal justice system.
Right. "Moles" usually say that they wanted to get as much intel as possible about the enemy (USA gov) and then bring the stuff to KGB.

Everybody wants to minimize the guilt, of course. But you to change the object 's behavior right away saying that the actual situation is : you didn't come to us - we had to stop your espionage activity and bring you here. You've been paid by____ for the treason, so stop the bullshit. Don't blame the government, your boss or your family situation. Tell the truth about what you did and you'll have much better chances at court".

.The Reid Nine Steps of Interrogation
1.The direct positive confrontation. Advise the suspect that the investigation clearly indicates that he is responsible for the commission of a crime.
Right.
That's important. The object MUST NOT DENY THE GUILT. He has to think and talk right away only about HOW TO MINIMIZE HIS GUILT. You have to get this first small small victory right away and break his strategy. Don't give him time to invent a new one, attack (bombard him with questions and evidence.

2. Theme development. Offer moral or psychological excuses for the suspect's criminal behavior.
Wrong. The suspect has to offer excuses himself and you have to either except them or not.

3-4. Statements the suspect makes during theme development. Most guilty suspects and all innocent ones will offer denials during theme development.
Wrong. You have to close the "gate" completely at the beginning of interrogation - no denial. That's very important - he can't say "I didn't do it".

5. To procure the suspect's attention to the theme. At this stage the investigator may move his chair in closer to the suspect's. A person who is physically close to another individual is also emotionally closer to that person. The investigator may also ask hypothetical

questions designed to stimulate internal thoughts from the suspect. For the first time during the interrogation, the suspect may begin to think about telling the truth. This is termed being in a "passive mood." The behavioral signs at this stage of an interrogation include dropped barriers (uncrossing arms or legs), a less tense posture, eye contact focused to the floor and sometimes tears.

Right.

No more pressure, you are not a friend, but you are a "good cop" who wants to understand, not to punish, and who wants to present the court with a true picture of a crime and THE SUSPECT'S PERSONALITY which is not bad, which is good because he has courage to tell the truth and start a new life.

6. Responding to the suspect's passive mood. The investigator condenses theme concepts to one or two central elements and moves into the next step of the process designed to elicit the initial admission of guilt.

Right.

What is "central element"? Admission that he was a member of a terrorist group, because then you can "open the box" and get the names, facts, plans, weapons, etc. Leave admission of the object's guilt for a desert.

7. Presenting an alternative question. Examples of an alternative question include, "Have you done this many times before or was this just the first time?" "Was this whole thing your idea or did you get talked into it?"

Right.

Same trick - help the object to minimize (not to deny!) his guilt to make him talk. My agent in the cell talks the object into admitting "one small episode and that's it - they gonna leave you alone". Next day I presented this "small episode" to other group members and in return he gave me everything he knew about my object. I came back , put the fact on the table: "What happened / We made a deal to be honest with each other ? What are you doing ? I want to help you , and now look what I got from your partner ! "

8. Developing the oral confession.
Right.
Don't smile no matter what he's saying and don't press - the car is going down the hill, don't push it.

9. The oral confession is converted to a court admissible document. A confession is a statement acknowledging personal responsibility for a crime including details only the guilty person would know.
Right.
That's the procedure. I have nothing to

# Part 3. HOMELAND SECURITY

U.S. NATIONAL STRATEGY FOR HOMELAND SECURITY 2007

Why it does not work

1."Homeland Security Defined. Homeland Security is a concerted national effort to prevent terrorist attacks within the United States, reduce America's vulnerability to terrorism, and minimize the damage and recover from attacks that do occur".

Wrong. Homeland security is the US government business, not national effort, aimed to prevent, fight , or minimize consequences of the proliferation of weapons of mass destruction, terrorism, natural disasters, pandemic diseases and other emergencies. We can't talk about terrorism seriously because FBI and CIA do not belong to the Homeland Security Department.

2."America is at war with terrorist enemies who are intent on attacking our Homeland and destroying our way of life".

Wrong. Statements where terrorists aim our way of life do not exist.

3."Our National Strategy for Homeland Security recognizes that…we must continue to focus on the persistent and evolving terrorist threat".

Wrong. "Persistent terrorist threat" means we have no idea what to do, how to do it and for how long.

4."It [the Strategy] provides a common framework by which our entire Nation should focus its efforts on

the following four goals:
-prevent and disrupt terrorist attacks;
-protect the American people, our critical structure, and key resources;
-respond to and recover from incidents that do occur;
-continue to strengthen the foundation to ensure our long-term success."

Wrong. These are the government functions, "entire Nation" has nothing to do with them.

4. "The terrorist attacks on September 11, 2001, were acts of war against the United States and the principles of freedom, opportunity, and openness that define the American way of life".

Wrong. If a terrorist group attacks the most powerful country in the world , and the government calls it "war", we have no government.

5. "The Federal Government as a united whole – and not simply one or two departments or agencies - has a critical role in homeland security and leads in those areas... These areas include, for example, intelligence missions; and detecting, tracking, and rendering safe weapons of mass destruction (WMD).

Wrong. That's a joke . Homeland Security Department generously shares its responsibility with all other departments and agencies. Perfect – no responsibility . Besides, FBI and CIA are not included in this department – how the hell are you going to plan and complete intelligence missions and detect WMD ?! Responsibility dispersed – that's the name of the game we, the Nation, pay for !

6. "As the country's principal providers of goods and services, and the owners or operators of approximately 85 % of the Nation's critical infrastructure, business have both an

interest in and responsibility for ensuring their own security ".
Wrong. Another joke. How the hell can we, regular American people, protect ourselves against professional , secret, very well funded, trained and armed terrorist organizations ?! We don't even have to think about it and we don't care – we pay taxes and we demand security from the government which is, unfortunately, a joke !

7. "In order to complete this truly national effort, we also must encourage and draw upon an informed and active citizenry. For instance, citizens should each understand what to do if they observe suspicious behavior in their community".

Wrong. For years I enjoy "See something, say something" NYPD posters all over NYC subway stations. For years cops ask to show the bags at those stations. Knives, guns, drugs – not even a single terrorist found. Do I have to explain that terrorism is a secret professional job ?

8. "Since September 11, we have made extraordinary progress, with most of our important successes in the War on Terror".

Wrong. We can't win war on terror, because the world is totally anti-American. Now.

9. "The FBI and the Department of Justice have made the prevention of terrorist attacks their highest priority".

Wrong. Russian and Chinese political espionage and has to be their highest priority !

10. "Terrorists have declared their intention tp acquire and use weapons of mass destruction (WMD).

Wrong. Nobody declared hat.

11. "We also must never lose sight of al-Qaida's persistent desire for weapons of mass destruction, as the group continues to try to acquire and use chemical, biological, radiological, or nuclear material".

Wrong. There are no facts on that. Pay attention to "or nuclear material" – another joke.

12. Hizballah may increasingly consider attacking the Homeland if it perceives the United States as posing a direct threat to the group or Iran, its principal sponsor.

Wrong. Hizballah is already the U.S.-designated terrorist organization (and a direct threat to us) – why they are not attacking us ?

13. "Al-Qaida's plotting against our Homeland, for instance, focuses on prominent political, economic, and infrastructure targets designed to produce mass casualties, visually dramatic destruction, significant economic damage, fear, and loss of confidence in government among our population.

Wrong. Al-Qaida already did all of that on September 11, 2007, and there's no need to repeat the action to show how vulnerable and unprotected we are.

14. "In order to prevent and disrupt terrorist attacks in the United States, we are working to prevent the emergence of violent Islamic radicalization in order to deny terrorists future recruits and defeat homegrown extremism".

Wrong. Too late.

15. "By preventing terrorists from entering the United States, we hinder their ability to identify and surveil possible targets, conduct planning, and launch an attack within our Homeland".

Wrong. Terrorists recruit American citizens who live, work or travel abroad, if they can't enter the United States.

16. "In order to uncover terrorists and terrorist activity against the backdrop of our highly mobile dynamic, and diverse society, we must attain domain awareness of the actions, events, and trends that occur throughout our land, maritime, air, space, and cyber domains. This is a multi-

faceted process".

Wrong. For that you have to change democracy into totalitarian rule where the state regulates every aspect of private and public life ,and restricts civil rights and initiates mass surveillance.

17."Recognizing that the future is uncertain and that we cannot envision or prepare for every potential threat, we must understand and accept a certain level of risk as a permanent condition".

Wrong. The future is absolutely certain ! We have a definite set of threats : natural disasters, like hurricanes, tornadoes or earthquakes, we have a nuclear power plant emergency, pandemic diseases, proliferation of WMD and terrorism. What is uncertain about preparing for these threats ?!

We MUST "prepare for every potential threat", am I clear ?

18."Our deterrent strategy – making it increasingly difficult for our enemies to achieve their objective of an attack in the Homeland by denying them and their weapons entry to the United States, denying them the ability to operate effectively within our borders, and denying them future recruits by preventing them homegrown radicalization".

Wrong. I don't see problems with buying illegal guns inside USA.

19. "Our entire Nation shares common responsibilities in homeland security".

Wrong. Don't turn the table. We do not want to share responsibilities with the government. We pay taxes – that's enough.

20."Since the turn of the millennium, our Nation has endured history's deadliest attack of international terrorism and the most destructive natural disaster to strike American soil. In the face of these challenges, America has responded courageously, with focus and clarity of purpose, and today we are safer, stronger and better prepared to address the full range of catastrophic events, including man- made natural disasters."

Wrong. Hurricane Katrina (2005), one of the most deadliest (1,836 lives) and costliest ($81,2 billion) in American history, proved we have chaos instead of homeland security. Let's wait for another category 3 hurricane to see if I'm wrong.

## U.S. NATIONAL INFRASTRUCTURE PROTECTION PLAN 2006
### Why it does not work

1."Future terrorist attacks against critical infrastructure (CI) across the United States could seriously threaten national security, result in mass casualties, weaken the economy and damage public morale and confidence".

Wrong. If terrorists could seriously threaten national security, we have serious problems with national security which means emergency situation. If terrorists could damage our morale, we are not the nation. Besides, you implant panic and you, not terrorists, damage public confidence.

2."It is not practical or feasible to protect all assets, systems and networks against every possible terrorist attack vector".

Wrong. If we have a national security system we must protect everything and everybody from terror. If we do not have it, we have to create and use it "against every possible terrorist vector".

3."Department of Homeland Security does not have broad regulatory authority over critical infrastructure and cannot compel private sector entities to submit infrastructure or operational information. Rather, DHS works in partnership with industry to identify the necessary information and promote the trusted exchange of such data".

Wrong. Department of Homeland Security must have absolute access to any information if it is vital to national security.

4."Terrorists may contemplate attacks against the Nation's critical infrastructure to achieve three general types of effects:

-direct infrastructure effects: disruption or arrest of critical functions through direct attacks on an asset, system or network

Wrong. You cannot attack directly the system or network, because it's protected by multilevel security system. If it's not protected, it's a small target of no interest.

-indirect infrastructure effects: cascading disruption and financial consequences for the society and economy through public and private sector reactions to an attack

Wrong. What public reaction has financial consequences for the society ? That's just stupid.

-exploitation of infrastructure: exploitation of elements of a particular infrastructure to disrupt or destroy another target or produce cascading consequences

Wrong. Terrorists do not need that; all they need is media attention and any explosion with minimum casualties is enough for that.

5."As security measures around more predictable targets increase, terrorists are likely to shift their focus to less protected targets".

Wrong. We do not have less protected targets in America. If we have them, Department of Homeland Security does not exist.

## GET READY FOR DISASTER

What to do first:
-decide where you should meet your household members in case somebody is lost
-make sure everyone knows the address and phone number of your second meeting place
-know all exit routes from your home and neighborhood
-designate an out of state friend or relative that household members can call if separated during disaster
-account for everybody's needs, especially seniors, people with disabilities, and non-English speakers

What to take:
-copies of your ID's in a waterproof and portable container
-extra set of car and house keys
-credit and ATM cards and cash in small bills
-bottled water and non-perishable food such as energy bars
-flashlight, battery-operated radio, extra batteries
-medication for at least one weak
-first-aid kit
-sturdy, comfortable shoes, lightwear raingear, blanket
-child care supplies or other special care items

What to have in your home:
-one gallon of drinking water per person per day
-canned foods and manual can-opener
-first-aid kit, medications and prescriptions
-flashlight, battery-operated radio
-whistle
-iodine tablets or one quart of unscented bleach (for disinfecting water ONLY if directed to do so by health

officials) and eyedropper (for adding bleach to water)
-personal hygiene items
-sturdy shoes, heavy gloves, warm clothes, a blanket, lightweight raingear
-extra fire extinguisher, smoke detectors, carbon monoxide detectors
-mobile phone
-child care supplies or other special care items

Be prepared to evacuate:
-if there is time, secure your home: close and lock windows and doors, and unplug appliances before you leave
-remember, evacuation routes change based on the emergency, so stay tuned to the local news

If you are asked to shelter in place:
-go inside your home or the nearest appropriate facility (school, library, church, etc.)
-take shelter in a room that has few doors and windows.
-seal all doors and windows
-turn off all ventilation systems
-do not used the phone – keep the phone line available for emergency calls
-stay tuned to your radio or TV for emergency information and updates
-if you can, try to seek shelter with friends or relatives outside the affected area

Utilities disruptions:
-if you smell gas: do not smoke or light lighter or matches, do not operate any light switches or electrical devices;
-open windows; evacuate immediately and call 911

-if there's a power outage: call your power provider; disconnect or turn off all appliances that would otherwise go on automatically when service is restored. If several appliances start up at once, they may overload the electric circuits; stay indoors if possible. Never touch or go near downed power lines, even if you think they are safe; keep a battery-operated radio on for updates on the restoration process; if you lose power and/or heat in the winter, insulate home as much as possible; do not use generators indoors – without proper ventilation they can create deadly carbon monoxide

Extremely hot weather:
-stay out of the sun, drink plenty of non-alcoholic, not-caffeinated fluids, consider going to public pools and air-conditioned stores and moles, or cooling centers; never leave children or those who require special care in a parked car

Earthquake:
-drop to the floor
-take cover under a solid piece of furniture or next to an interior wall, cover your head and neck with your arms
-use a doorway for shelter only if it is in close proximity to you and if you know it is a strongly supported
-stay inside until shaking stops and it is safe to go outside. Research has shown that most injuries occur when people inside buildings attempt to move to a different location inside the building or try to leave
-DO NOT use the elevators
-if outdoors: stay there, move away from buildings, streetlights and utility wires. Once in the open, stay there until the shaking stops. The greatest danger exists directly outside buildings, at exits, and alongside exterior walls. Ground

movement during an earthquake is seldom the direct cause of death or injury. Most earthquake-related casualties result from collapsing walls, flying glass, and falling objects.

-if in a moving vehicle: stop as quickly as safety permits and stay in the vehicle. Avoid stopping near or under buildings, trees, overpasses and utility wires. Proceed cautiously once the earthquake has stopped. Avoid roads, bridges or ramps that might have been damaged by the earthquake.

-be prepared for after-shocks , which often follow an earthquake

Flood:
-be aware of streams, drainage channels, canyons, and other areas known to flood suddenly. Flash floods can occur in these areas with or without such typical warnings as rain clouds or heavy rain.

-if you must prepare to evacuate, secure your home, bring in outdoor furniture, move essential items to an upper floor. Turn off utilities at the main switches or valves if instructed to do so, disconnect electrical appliances, do not touch electrical equipment if you are wet or standing in the water.

-if you have to leave your home: do not walk through moving water (six inches of moving water can make you fall). Use a stick to check the firmness of the ground in front of you. Do not drive into flooded areas. If floodwaters rise around your car, abandon the car and move to higher ground if you can do so safely. You and the vehicle can be quickly swept away.

Remember: six inches of water will reach the bottom of most passenger cars causing loss of control and possible stalling. A foot of water will float many vehicles. Two feet of rushing water can carry away most vehicles including sport utility vehicles (SUV's) and pick-ups.

Hurricane.

A hurricane is a type of tropical cyclone, the generic term for a low pressure system that generally forms in the tropics. A typical cyclone is accompanied by thunderstorms, and in the Northern Hemisphere, a counter-clock circulation of winds near the earth's surface. All Atlantic and Gulf of Mexico coastal areas are subject to hurricanes or tropical storms. Parts of the Southwest United States and the Pacific Coast experience heavy rains and floods each year from hurricanes spawned off Mexico. The Atlantic hurricane season lasts from June to November, with the peak season from mid-August to late October. Hurricanes can cause catastrophic damage to coastlines and several hundred miles inland. Winds can exceed 155 miles per our. Hurricanes and tropical storms can also spawn tornadoes and microbursts, create storm surges along the coast, and cause extensive damage from heavy rainfall. Hurricanes are classified into five categories based on their wind speed, central pressure, and damage potential. Category 3 and higher hurricanes are considered major hurricanes, though categories 1 and 2 are still extremely dangerous and warrant your full attention. Hurricanes can produce widespread torrential rains, floods are the deadly and destructive result. Slow moving storms and tropical storms moving into mountainous regions tend o produce especially heavy rain. Excessive rain can trigger landslides or mud slides, especially in mountainous regions.

If you live in a mobile home or temporary structure – such shelters are particularly hazardous during hurricanes no matter how well fastened to the ground. If you live in a high-rise building – hurricane winds are stronger at higher elevations. If you live on the coast, on a floodplain, near a river, or on an inland waterway. If you are unable to evacuate, stay indoors during the hurricane and away from windows and glass doors, close all interior doors, keep curtains and blinds closed, take refuge in a small interior room, closet, or hallway on the lowest level.

Hurricane categories.

Scale number Sustained winds Hurricane scale Storm surge

(category) (MPH)

1 74-95 Minimal: unanchored mobile homes, vegetation and 4-5 feet

signs.

2 96-110 Moderate: all mobile homes, roofs, small crafts 6-8 feet

flooding.

3 111-130 Extensive: small buildings, low-lying roads cut-off. 9-12 feet

4 131-155 Extreme: roofs destroyed, trees down, roads cut-off,

mobile homes destroyed. Beach homes flooded. 13-18 feet

5 more than 155 Catastrophic: most buildings destroyed. Vegetation

destroyed. Greater than 18 feet

Volcano.

If volcano erupts where you live: follow the evacuation order issued by authorities and evacuate immediately from the volcano area to avoid flying debris, hot gases, lateral blast, and lava flow. Be aware of mudflows – they can move faster than you can walk or run. Look upstream before crossing a bridge, and do not cross the bridge if a mudflow is approaching. Avoid river valleys and low-lying areas. If you have a respiratory ailment, avoid contact with any amount of ash; use a dust mask or hold a damp cloth over your face to help with breathing. Stay away from areas downwind from the volcano to avoid volcanic ash. Stay indoors until the ash has settled unless there is a danger of the roof collapsing. Close doors, windows and all ventilation in the house (chimney vents, furnaces, air conditioners, fans. Clear heavy ash from flat or low-pitched roofs and rain gutters. Avoid running car or truck engines – driving car stir up volcanic ash that can clog engines, damage moving parts, and stall vehicles. Avoid diving in heavy ash fall unless absolutely required. If you have to drive, keep peed down to 35 MPH or slower.

Tornado.
Tornadoes are nature's most violent storms. Spawned from powerful thunderstorms, tornadoes can cause fatalities and devastate neighborhood in seconds. A tornado appears as a rotating, funnel-shaped cloud that extends from a thunderstorm to the ground with whirling winds that can reach 300 MPH. Damage paths can be in excess of 1 mile wide and 50 miles long. Every state is at some risk from this hazard. Tornadoes generally occur near the trailing edge of a thunderstorm.

During tornado go to a pre-designated shelter area such as a safe room, basement, storm cellar, or the lowest building level. If there is o basement, go to the center of an interior room on the lowest level (closet, interior hallway) away from corners, windows, doors and outside walls. Get under a sturdy table and use your arms to protect your head and neck; do not open windows. If you are inside a vehicle, trailer or mobile home, get out immediately and go to the lowest floor of a sturdy, nearby building or a storm shelter. If you are outside with no shelter, lie flat in a nearby ditch and cover your head with your hands. Be aware of the potential for flooding. Do not get under overpass or bridge – you are safer in a low, flat location. Never try to outran tornado in urban or congested areas in a car or truck; instead, leave the vehicle immediately for safe shelter. Watch out for flying debris – they cause most fatalities and injuries.

Tsunami.

Tsunamis are a series of enormous waves created by an underwater disturbance such as an earthquake, landslide, volcanic eruption, or meteorite. A tsunami can move hundreds of MPH in the open ocean and smash into land with waves as high as 100 feet or more. The most destructive tsunamis have occurred along the coasts of California, Oregon, Washington, Alaska and Hawaii. Aras are at greater risk if they are less than 25 feet above sea level and within 1 mile of the shoreline. Drowning id the most common cause of death associated with a tsunami. Tsunami waves are very destructive to structures in the run-up zone. Other hazards include flooding, contamination of drinking water, and fires from gas lines or ruptured tanks.

Before and during a tsunami: turn on your radio to learn if there is a tsunami warning if an earthquake occurs and you are in a coastal area. Move inland to higher ground immediately and stay there. Stay away from the beach; never go down to the beach to watch a tsunami come in- if you can see the wave you are too close to escape it ! If there is noticeable recession in water away from the shoreline his is nature's tsunami warning and it should be heeded. You should move away immediately.

Thunderstorm.
If you are in the forest, seek shelter in a low area under

a thick growth of small trees. In an open area, go to a low place such as a ravine or valley; be alert for flash floods. Go to land and find shelter immediately if you are on the open water. Anywhere you feel your hair stand on end (which indicates that lightning is about to strike), squat low to the ground on the balls of your feet; place your hands over your ears and your head between your knees; make yourself the smallest target possible and minimize your contact with the ground; do not lie flat on the ground.

Building collapses or explosions :
-if you are in a building: get out as quickly as possible
-if you can't get out of the building : get under a sturdy table or desk
-if you are trapped by debris: cover your nose and mouth with a cloth or clothing
-move around as little as possible to avoid kicking up dust, which is harmful to inhale; if possible, use a flashlight;
 -tap on a pipe or wall so rescuers can hear where you are; shout only as a last resort as shouting can cause you to inhale dangerous amounts of dust

Hazardous materials or chemical spills:
-stay upwind of the material if possible
-seek medical attention as soon as possible if needed
-if there's event indoors, try to get out of the building without passing the contaminated area
 -if exposed, remove outer layer of clothes, separate yourself from them, and wash yourself

A parcel or letter may be considered suspicious if there is :
-handwritten or poorly typed address, incorrect titles or

titles with no name, or misspelling of common words
-addressed to someone no longer with your organization or not addressed to a specific person
-strange return address or no return address
-marked with restrictions, such as "Personal", "Confidential", or "Do not X-ray"
-excessive postage
-powderly substance on the outside
-unusual weight given its size, lopsided, or oddly shaped
-unusual amount of tape on it
-odors, discoloration or oily stains
If you receive a suspicious package or envelope:
-put it down – preferably on a stable surface
-cover it with an airtight container like a trash can or plastic bag
-call 911 and alert your building's security officials
-alert others to the presence of the package and evacuate the area
-wash your hands with soap and water if you have handed the package

Nuclear power plant emergency.
  Nuclear power plants use the heat generated from nuclear fission in a contained environment to convert water to steam, which powers generators to produce electricity. They produce about 20% of the nation's power; nearly 3 million Americans live within 10 miles of an operating power plant. Although the construction and operation of these facilities are closely monitored and regulated by the Nuclear Regulatory Commission (NRC), accidents are possible. An accident could result in dangerous levels of radiation that could affect the health and safety of the public living nearby. Local and state

governments, federal agencies, and the electric utilities have emergency response plans in the event of a nuclear power plant incident. The plans define two emergency planning zones. One zone covers an area within a 10-mile radius of the plant, where it is possible that people could be harmed by direct radiation exposure. The second zone covers a broader area, usually up to a 50-mile radius from the plant, where radioactive materials could contaminate water supplies, food crops, and livestock.

The potential danger from an accident at a nuclear power plant is exposure to radiation. This exposure could come from the release of radioactive material from the plant into the environment, usually characterized by a plume (cloud-like formation) of radioactive gases and particles. The major hazards to people in the vicinity of the plume are:

-radiation exposure to the body from the cloud and particles deposited on the ground

-inhalation of radioactive materials

-ingestion of radioactive materials

Radioactive materials are composed of atoms that are unstable. An unstable atom gives off its excess energy until it becomes stable. The energy emitted is radiation, and it has a cumulative effect: the longer a person is exposed to radiation, the greater the effect. Terms to help identify a nuclear power plant emergency are:

-notification of unusual event. No radiation leak is expected, no action on your part will be necessary.

-alert. A small problem has occurred, and small amounts of radiation could leak inside the plant. This will not affect you and no action is required.

-site area emergency: area sirens may be sounded ;listen to your radio or TV for safety information

-general emergency. Radiation could leak outside the plant and off the plant site. The sirens will sound. Tune to your local radio or TV for reports. Be prepared to follow instructions promptly.

During a nuclear power plant emergency:
If you are told to evacuate: keep car windows and vents closed; use re-circulating air.
If you are told to remain indoors:
-turn off the air conditioner, ventilation fans, furnace and other air in-takers
-go to a basement or other underground area, if possible
-do not use the telephone unless absolutely necessary
If you expect you have been exposed to nuclear radiation:
-change clothes and shoes
-put exposed clothing in a plastic bag
-seal the bag and place it out of the way
-take a thorough shower
Keep food in covered containers or in the refrigerator ( food not previously covered should be washed before being put in to containers).

Learn from Chernobyl (Ukraine) nuclear power plant explosion.

The explosion in reactor #4 at the Chernobyl nuclear power station (Ukraine) took place on April 26, 1986, during a test. The operating crew planed to test whether the turbines could produce sufficient energy to keep the coolant pumps running in the event of a loss of power until the emergency diesel generator was activated. In order to prevent the test run of the reactor being interrupted, the safety systems were deliberately switched off. For the test, the reactor had to be powered down to 25% of its capacity. This procedure did not go according to a plan: for unknown reasons, the reactor power level fell less that 1%. The power therefore had to be slowly increased. But 30 seconds after the start of the test, there was a sudden and unexpected power surge. The reactor's emergency shutdown (which should have halted the chain reaction) failed. Within fractions of a second, the power level and temperature rose many times over, the reactors went out of control. There was a violent explosion, and the 1000-tonne sealing cap on the reactor building was blown off. At temperatures of over 2000' C, the fuel rods melted. The graphite covering of the reactor then ignited; in the ensuing inferno, the radioactive fission products released during the core meltdown were sucked up into the atmosphere. Determining causes of accident was not easy, because there was no experience of comparable events to refer to. The cause of the accident is still described as imperfect technology.

Next day, the 45 000 inhabitants of Pripyat, 4 km away, were evacuated in buses; the town remains uninhabited to this day. Within 10 days, 130 000 people from 76 settlements in 30 km area around the reactor were evacuated. The territory has been declared an exclusion zone. On May 23, 1986, far too late from a medical point of view, the official distribution of iodine pills began, ( to prevent the absorption of radioactive iodine by the thyroid, but the greatest proportion of radioactive iodine had already been released in the first ten days following the explosion). According to the Chernobyl Forum Report (2005) the deaths of 47 liquidators (who were clearing up in Chernobyl) between 1986 and 2005 can be directly attributed to high radiation exposure. Of the 200 000 liquidators who worked on the reactor in te first year after the explosion, a total of 2200 may eventually die owing to the consequences of radiation exposure. Other reports claim that 800 000 liquidators are endangered. They suffered and suffer (as do other survivors) from conditions including lung cancer and leukemia, cardiovascular diseases and inflammation of the digestive tract.

I remember this horrible situation perfectly well and I knew it from inside, because at the time I worked for KGB. Nobody knew nothing, civil defense system did not work, the government was in a shock, people – in panic. Families were running in every direction or sending kids to faraway relatives. For a week situation was out of control. Nuclear scientists had nothing to say or predict.

Nuclear blast.

A nuclear blast is an explosion with intense light and heat, a damaging pressure wave, and widespread radioactive material that can contaminate the air, water and ground services for miles around. A nuclear device can range from a weapon carried by an intercontinental missile launched by a hostile nation , to small portable nuclear devise transported by an individual. All nuclear devices cause deadly effects when exploded, including:
-blinding light
-intense heat ( thermal radiation)
-initial nuclear radiation
-blast
-fires started by the heat pulse
-secondary fire caused by the destruction

The extent, nature , and arrival of these hazards are difficult to predict. The geographical dispersion of hazard effects will be defined by the:

-size of the device

-height above the ground the device was detonated (this will determine the extent of blast effects)

-nature of the surface beneath the explosion – flat areas are more susceptible to blast effects

-existing meteorological conditions (wind speed and direction will affect arrival of fallout; precipitation may wash fallout from the atmosphere

Even if individuals are not close enough to the nuclear blast to be affected by the direct impacts, they may be affected by radioactive fallout. Any nuclear blast results in some fallout, blasts that occur near the earth's surface create much greater amounts of fallout than blasts that occur at higher altitudes. This is because the tremendous heat produced from a nuclear blast causes an up-draft of air that forms the mushroom cloud. When a blast occurs near the earth's surface, millions of vaporized dirt particles are also drawn into the cloud. As the heat diminishes, radioactive materials that have vaporized condense on the particles and fall back to surface – this is a radioactive fallout. The fallout material decays over a long period of time, and is the main source of residual nuclear radiation. Fallout from a nuclear explosion may be carried by wind currents for hundreds of miles if the right conditions exist. Effects from even a small portable device exploded at ground level can be potentially deadly.

Nuclear radiation cannot be seen, smelled, or otherwise detected by normal senses. Radiation can only be detected by radiation monitoring devices. This makes radiological emergencies different from other types of emergencies, such as floods or hurricanes. Monitoring can project the fallout arrival times, which will be announced through official warning channels. However, any increase in surface build-up of gritty dust and dirt should be a warning for taking protective measures.

In addition to other effects, a nuclear weapon detonated in or above the earth's atmosphere can create an electromagnetic pulse (EMP), a high –density electrical field. An EMP acts like a stroke of lightning but is stronger, faster and shorter. An EMP can seriously damage electronic devices connected to power sources or antennas. This includes communication systems, computers, electrical appliances and automobile or aircraft ignition systems; the damage could range from a minor interruption to actual turnout of components. Most electronic equipment within 1,000 miles of a high-altitude nuclear detonation could be affected. Although an EMP is unlikely to harm most people, it could harm those with pacemakers or other implanted electronic devices.

During a nuclear blast:

-if attack warning is issued, take cover as quickly as you can, below ground if possible, and stay there until instructed to do otherwise; listen for official information and follow instructions

-if you are caught outside and unable to get inside immediately: do not look at the flash or fireball – it can blind you; take cover behind anything that might offer protection; lie flat on the ground and cover your head – if the explosion is some distance away, it could take 30 seconds or more for the blast wave to hit; take shelter as soon as you can, even if you are many miles from ground zero where the attack occurred – radioactive fallout can be carried by the wind for hundreds of miles.

Remember the three protective factors: distance, shielding, time.

Radiological dispersion device (RDD).

Terrorist use of an RDD ( often called "dirty bomb") is considered far more likely than use of a nuclear explosive device. An RDD combines a conventional explosive device – such as a bomb – with radioactive material. It is designed to scatter dangerous and sub-lethal amounts of radioactive materials over a general area. Such RDDs appeal to terrorists because they require limited technical knowledge to build and deploy compared to a nuclear device. Also, the radioactive materials in RDDs are widely used in medicine, agriculture, industry and research, and are easier to obtain than weapons grade uranium or plutonium.

The primary purpose of terrorist use of an RDD is to cause psychological fear and economic disruption. Some devices could cause fatalities from exposure to radioactive materials. Depending on the speed at which the area of the RDD detonation was evacuated or how successful people were at sheltering-in-place, the number of deaths and injuries from an RDD might not be substantially greater than from a conventional explosion. The size of the affected area and the level of destruction caused by an RDD would depend on the sophistication and size of the conventional bomb, the type of radioactive material used, the quality and quantity of the radioactive material, and the local meteorological conditions – primarily wind and precipitation. The area affected could be placed off-limits to the public for several months during cleanup efforts.

Chemical attack.

If you are instructed to remain in your home or office building:

-close doors and windows and turn off all ventilation,

including furnaces, air conditioners
-seek shelter in an internal room and take your disaster supplies kit
-seal the room with duct tape and plastic sheeting
-listen to your radio for instructions from authorities
If you are caught in or near a contaminated area, you should:
-move away immediately in a direction upwind of the source
-find a shelter as quickly as possible

## TERRORISM

Terrorism is the unlawful use of violence against people or property to coerce or intimidate governments or societies, often to achieve political, religious or ideological objectives. It's also a form of unconventional and psychological warfare. The common strategy of terrorists is to commit acts of violence. Terrorism is a political tactic. "Red" terror is aimed against certain politicians; "black" refers more to mass murders. The two can be mixed.

Purposes: to scare the nation, neutralize the government and show its inability to rule the country; to make the government admit that terror organization is a real political power; to draw media and public (international) attention to a certain political problem, to provoke the government to use military force and start civil war; to prove some political or religious ideology; prevent or delay important political decisions or legislation; discourage foreign investments or foreign government assistance programs; change the government through revolution or civil war.

Types of terrorism:

Civil disorders – a form of collective violence interfering with the peace, security and normal functioning of the community.

Political terrorism – violent criminal behavior designed primarily to generate fear in the nation for political purposes..

Non-political terrorism – terrorism that is not aimed at political purposes but which exhibits conscious design to create and maintain high degree of fear for coercive purposes, but the end is individual or collective gain rather than the achievement of a political objective.

Official or state terrorism – referring to nations whose rule is based upon fear and oppression that reach similar to terrorism or such proportions. It also may be referred to as structural terrorism defined broadly as terrorist acts carried out by governments in pursuit of political objectives, often as part of their foreign policy.

Terrorist objectives.

1.Recognition

At the outset of a terrorist campaign, the objective of terrorist acts may be national or international recognition of a cause. The reasons for seeking recognition might also include attracting recruits, obtaining funds, or demonstrating strength. Groups seeking recognition require events that have high probability of attracting media attention. Specific incidents may be suicide bombing in public place (e.g. a green market), hijacking of an aircraft, the kidnapping of a politician or other prominent person, the seizing of occupied buildings (schools, hospitals) or other hostage barricade situations. Once they gain attention, the terrorists may demand that political statement be disseminated. .

2. Coercion.

Coercion is the attempt to force a desired behavior by individuals, groups, or governments. This objective calls for a strategy of a very selective targeting which rely on publicly announced bombings, destruction of property and other acts which are initially less violent than the taking of human life. Contemporary examples include the bombing of corporate headquarters and banking facilities with little or no loss of life.

3. Intimidation.

Intimidation differs from coercion. Intimidation attempts to prevent individuals or groups from acting: coercion attempts to force actions. Terrorists may use intimidation to reduce the effectiveness of security forces by making them afraid to act. Intimidation can discourage competent citizens from seeking or accepting positions within the government. The threat of violence can also keep the general public from taking part in important political activities such as voting. As in the case of coercion, terrorists use a strategy of selective targeting although they may intend the targets to look as though they were chosen indiscriminately.

4. Provocation.

The specific objective is to provoke overreaction on the part of government forces. The strategy normally calls for attacking targets symbolic of the government (for example, Twin Towers in NYC). Attacks of this type demonstrate vulnerability to terrorist acts and contribute to a loss of confidence in the government's ability to provide security.

Factors that may contribute to terrorism:
high population growth rates.
high unemployment
legging economies

extremism
ethnic conflict
religious conflict
territorial conflict

Organization and tactic.

Organized terror is "organized construction":
-search and recruitment of people (active and passive supporters), including informants and supporters in government agencies, counterintelligence and police
-getting money (robberies, illegal operations with drugs and weapons, legal business, searching for donors with the same political views)
-security system, including a system of "cells" or small groups (some groups may organize multifunctional cells that combine several skills into one tactical unit). Preparing places where members can hide, relax, get medical care; keep weapons, money, special literature. System also includes fake IDs and counter-intelligence (detection of traitors, preventing collapse of the group and uncontrolled criminal activity (robberies)
-training camps (shooting, working with explosives). If the group is state supported or directed, the leadership usually includes one or more members who have been trained and educated by the sponsoring state
-"brainwashing" sessions (the group may include professional terrorists for hire who are not necessarily ideologically motivated)
-planning the actions
-making special connections with other groups and mafia

The typical terrorist organization is pyramidal. This format takes more people to support operations than to carry them out. Therefore, the majority of people who work in terrorist organizations serve to keep terrorists in the field. The most common job in terrorist groups is support, not combat.

Usually, organization is divided into 4 levels:

1st level. Command level. The smallest, most secret group at the top, not always openly free to communicate openly with other members.

2nd level. Active cadre. Responsible for carrying out the mission of the terrorist organization. Depending on the organization's size, each terrorist in the cadre may have one or more specialties. Other terrorists support each specialty, but the active cadre is the striking arm of the terrorist group. After the command structure, the cadre of active terrorists is the smallest organization in most terrorist structures.

3rd level. Active supporters. The active supporters are critical to terrorist operations. Any group can carry out a bombing, but to maintain a campaign of bombings takes support. Active supporters keep the terrorists in the field. They maintain communication channels, provide safe houses, gather intelligence. This is the largest internal group in the organization, and one which can be effectively countered by economic measures.

4th level. Passive supporters. This group is extremely difficult to identify and characterize because supporters do not readily join terrorist groups. In fact, they will likely deny any involvement. Many times they are used without their own knowledge, and often, they simply represent a favorable element of the political climate. When a terrorist group can muster political support, it will have a relatively large number of passive supporters. When its cause alienates the mainstream, passive support dwindles. Passive support complements active support, and again, this is a part of the organization which can be effectively countered by economic measures.

Most terrorist groups number fewer than 50 people and are incapable of mounting a long-term campaign. Under the command of only a few people, the group is divided according to specific tasks. Intelligence sections are responsible for assessing targets and planning operations. Support sections provides the means necessary to carry out the assault, and the tactical units are responsible for the actual terrorist action.

Terrorist organizations tend to have two primary types of subunits: a cell and a column. The cell is the most basic type. Composed of 4 to 6 people, the cell usually has a mission specialty, but it my be a tactical cell or an intelligence section. In some organizations, the duties of tactical cells very with the assignment. Other cells may exist as support wing.

Sometimes groups of cells will form to create columns. Columns are semiautonomous conglomerations of cells with a variety of specialties and a separate command structure. As combat units, columns have questionable effectiveness. They are usually too cumbersome to be used in major operations, and the secrecy demanded by terrorism prevents effective inter-column cooperation. Hence, columns are most often found fulfilling a function of combat support.

There's no other really effective way to fight terror but to recruit informants and construct a total surveillance web to control the nation in every way.

## Methods.

Hostage-taking.

This is usually an overt seizure of one or more people to gain publicity, concessions , or ransom in return for the release of the hostage or hostages. You must always negotiate if hostages have been taken. Negotiation produces some advantages for you. These advantages are: (a) the longer situation is prolonged, the more intelligence can be gathered on the location, motivation and identity, (b) the passage of time generally reduces anxiety, allowing the hostage taker to assess the situation rationally, (c) given enough time, the hostages may find a way to escape on their own, (c) the necessary resolve to kill or hold hostages lessens with timer, (d) terrorists may make mistakes. The negotiation team must have information to support negotiations (you get it from interviews with witnesses, escaped and released hostages, and captured suspects — it's very important to get the identities, personalities, motives, habits and abilities of the offenders).

One of the complications facing you in a siege involving hostages is the Stockholm syndrome where sometimes hostages can develop a sympathetic rapport with their captors. If this helps keep them safe from harm, this is considered to be a good thing, but there have been cases where hostages have tried to shield the captors during an assault or refused to co-operate with the authorities in bringing prosecutions. (In Britain if the siege involves perpetrators who are considered by the government to be terrorists, then if an assault is to take place, the civilian authorities hand command and control over to military).

Bombing.

Advantage of bombing includes it's attention-getting

capacity and the terrorist's ability to control casualties through time of detonation and placement of the device. The bomb is a popular weapon, because it is cheap to produce, easy to make, has variable uses, and is difficult to detect and trace after the action. In Iraq they usually use booby-trapped vehicles and car-bombs. A car bomb is an explosive device placed in a car or other vehicle and then exploded. It is commonly used as a weapon of assassination, terrorism or guerrilla warfare to kill the occupant(s) of the vehicle, people near the blast site, or to damage buildings or other property. Car bombs act as their own delivery mechanisms and can carry a relatively large amount of explosives without attracting suspicion. The earliest car bombs were intended for assassination. These were often wired to the car's ignition system - to explode when the car was started. Ignition triggering is now rare, as it is easy to detect and hard to install – interfering with the circuitry is time-consuming and car alarms can be triggered by drains on the car's electrical system. Also, the target may start the car remotely (inadvertently or otherwise), or the target may be a passenger a safe distance away when the car starts. It is now more common for assassination bombs to be affixed to the underside of the car and then detonated remotely or by the car motion. The bomb is exploded as the target approaches or starts the vehicle or, more commonly, after the vehicle begins to move, when the target is more likely to be inside. For this reason, security guards have to check the underside of vehicles with a long mirror mounted on a pole.

The effectiveness of a car bomb is that an explosion detonated inside a car is momentarily contained. If the force of explosion were to double each fraction of a second and the car were to contain the explosion for one second before its chassis gave way, this would result in a much greater force then if the detonation took place outside the car. Therefore a greater amount of damage is obtained from a given amount of explosive. Car bombs are also used by suicide bombers who seek to ram the car into a building and simultaneously detonate it. Defending against a car bomb involves keeping vehicles at a distance from vulnerable targets by using Jersey barriers, concrete blocks or by hardening buildings to withstand an explosion. Where major public roads pass near government buildings, road closures may be the only option (thus, the portion of Pennsylvania Avenue immediately behind the White house is closed to traffic. These tactics encourage potential bombers to target unprotected targets, such as markets.

Mass-casualty car bombing, and especially suicide car bombing, is widely used in Middle East, especially by Islamic fundamentalist group Hezbollah. The most notable car bombing (by Islamic Jihad)was the 1983 Beirut barracks bombing, which killed 241 U.S. marines and 48 French military personnel. In 1995, Timothy McVeigh detonated a Ryder box truck filled with an explosive mixture (fuel oil and fertilizer) in front of the Salfred P. Murrah Federal Building in Oklahoma City with 168 killed and over 800 injured. Iraqi insurgency often use car bombs against U.S. troops.

Suicide attack.

A major reason for the popularity of suicide attacks is tactical advantages over other types of terrorism. A terrorist can conceal weapons, make last-minute adjustments, infiltrate heavily guarded targets and he does not need a remote or delayed detonation, escape plans or rescue teams. Suicide attacks often target poorly- guarded, non-military facilities and personnel. .

Ambush and raid.

A well-planned ambush seldom fails. The terrorists have

time on their side, and can choose a suitable place. Raid (armed attack) on facilities usually have one of three purposes: to gain access to radio or TV stations (to make a public statement); to demonstrate the government's inability to guarantee the security of critical facilities; or to acquire money and weapons ( by bank pr armory robberies).

Assassination.

Assassination is the oldest terrorist tactic. Targets mostly are government officials, as well as the defectors from the terrorist group.

Kidnapping.

Kidnapping is usually a covert action and the perpetrators may not make themselves known for some time, while hostage –takers seek immediate publicity. Because of the time involved, a successful kidnapping requires elaborate planning and logistics, although the risk to the terrorists is less than in a hostage situation.

Sabotage.

Its objective is to demonstrate how vulnerable society is to the terrorists' actions on utilities, communications and transportation systems. In the more developed countries they are so interdependent that a serious disruption of one affects all and gains immediate public attention. Sabotage of industrial, commercial or military facilities is a tool to show

vulnerability of the target and the society while simultaneously making a statement or political, or monetary demand.

Hoaxes.

A threat against a person's life causes him and those around him to devote more time and effort to security measures. A bomb threat can close down a commercial building, empty a theater, or disrupt a transportation system at no cost to the terrorist. The longer-term effects of false alarms on the security forces are more dangerous than the temporary disruption of the hoax. Repeated threats that do not materialize dull the analytical and operational effectiveness of security personnel.

## COUNTERTERRORISM

Responses to terrorism include:
- laws, criminal procedures, deportations and enhanced police powers
-pre-emptive or reactive military action (military action can disrupt a terrorist group's operations temporarily, but it rarely ends the threat)
-increased intelligence (assets recruitment) and surveillance activities
-pre-emptive humanitarian activities
-more permissive interrogation and detention policies
-official acceptance of torture as a valid tool

You must gather the following information:

1.Group information.
Names, ideology (political or social philosophy), history of the group, dates significant to the group, and dates when former leaders have been killed or imprisoned (terrorist groups often strike on important anniversary dates).
2.Financial information.
Source of funds, proceeds from criminal activities, bank accounts information (sudden influxes of funding or bank withdrawals indicate preparation for activity). It's also important to determine the group's legal and financial supporters. Generally, anyone who would write an official

letter of protest or gather names on a petition for a terrorist is a legal supporter. Sometimes, an analysis of support will reveal linkages and mergers with other groups.

3.Personnel information.

List of leaders, list of members (and former members), any personnel connections with other groups of similar ideology. The skills of all group members (weapons expertise, electronics expertise) – knowing the skills of the group is an important part of threat assessment. If the philosophy revolves around one leader, it's important to know what will occur if something happens to that leader. Often, the analysis of family background is useful to determine how radically a leader or member was raised. Group structure, particularly if the organizational pattern is cellular, determines who knows whom.

As a group, terrorists are very team-oriented and always prepared for suicide missions. They are well-prepared for their mission , are willing to take risks and are attack-oriented. If captured, they will usually not confess or snitch on others as ordinary criminals do. Traditional law enforcement are not that effective when it comes to the investigation or intelligence of terrorism.

4.Location information.

Location of group's headquarters, location of group's "safe" houses (where they hide from authorities) and location of the group's "stash" houses (where they hide weapons and supplies). Regular attacks on "stash" houses is the most frequently used counterterrorism technique). It' important to specify the underground that exists where terrorists can flee. Terrorists like to live in communal homes instead of living alone.

Remember this:

1. Knowing just the functions of terrorism is a fight. Since terrorists are usually trying to provoke government's overreaction, anything the government can do to keep itself from overreacting works against them.

2. Since terrorists are usually trying to provoke government's overreaction, anything the government can do to keep itself from overreacting works against them. Since terrorists are trying to gain control of the media, anything on the part of the media which stifles exposure also stiles terrorism. Bombings make the best pictures (watch TV!), that's why terrorists use them mostly.

3. Terrorists often demand to release political prisoners, but this is never a true objective. The real trick is politization of all prisoners, the winning over of new recruits among the prison population.

4. Go after financial supporters of terrorism, not the terrorists themselves. .

5. Terrorists are imitators, not innovators. They often wait until some other group makes the first move. Most of them do this because they are sorely trying to imitate military strategy, others do it because of standardized paramilitary training or textbook lessons in guerrilla tactics, and still others do it to throw off suspicion from themselves.

6. The Stockholm Syndrome works in the favor of anti-terrorist forces. The longer the hostages stay alive, the less likelihood harm will come to them. With this syndrome, the hostages come to think of their captors as protecting them from the police and soon start to identify with their captors. The captors themselves start to develop a parent/child relationship with their hostages. Other syndromes include the Penelope

Syndrome , where women find violent criminals sexually attractive.

7. In assessing the threat of terrorism, it's important to concentrate on counting the number of incidents, not the number of victims or the value of harm. The only true comparison is the number of attacks since terrorists often have no idea themselves about how many victims will be killed by their actions. Nationalist groups tend to seek a high number of fatalities while revolutionary groups tend to seek fewer deaths and more wounds or injuries. Splinter or spin-off groups seem more interested in death counts and fatalities. The point is that no matter how many victims are targeted, the group is only a threat via its number of attacks as a percent of total activity.

8. Do count the number of victims saved by any preventive action. If you manage through some leverage to get the terrorist leader to stop things with a cease-fire agreement, regardless of whether further negotiation follows or not, it will help your agency if you have calculated how many lives you've saved, and can report this information to policymakers. Everyone wins by a cease-fire – the terrorist leaders look good, your leaders look good too. After the cease-fire, it's important to also measure the resumed level of violence and compare to pre-cease-fire levels.

9. Giving into terrorists' demands for political change only changes the pattern of violence , not violence itself. Economic and political reforms aimed at helping a certain group and resolving its grievances will win over some supporters among the general population, but in the long-run, will create new problems and a new set of grievances over the precise implementation of policy and the degree of power sharing. A much better strategy is to initiate economic and political reforms for all nation. Economic development solutions have

worked in Ireland, Uruguay and Italy.

10. The thing that works best is reduction of recruits, supplies and support. You have to reduce the number of active trainee members of the terrorist organization. Capture and imprisonment works (it has helped to keep Spain fairly terrorism-free), as well as preemptive strikes against training camps. The number of terrorists captured or killed should be counted, and this can be put as the denominator in a fraction with the number of government security forces killed in the numerator. You've also got to keep weapons, ammo and supplies out of hands of terrorists by destruction of their "stash" houses. Unfortunately, many religious terrorist groups operate under the cover of religion and blowing up religious buildings has a strong negative effect.

11. Terrorism does not respond to coalition-based sanctions which are intended to express the international community's disregard for them. Terrorist actually want their enemies to wage a war on terrorism because this gives them some pseudo-legitimacy that they are soldiers-at war. If they are broken up from receiving any psychological rewards or sympathy from their social support groups, this strategy might work.

12. Sharing of information and intelligence by counter-terrorism agents is essential. But there's always a threat, that a secret source might be "burnt out" during such "sharing".

13. Terrorist groups with a cell structure are most likely to thwart human intelligence since the purpose of the cell structure is to prevent any members from knowing who is the immediate leader. This may or may not be true with some groups (like the IRA) which mix family with business, depending upon levels of fidelity. The best approach for such groups may electronic surveillance. However, groups with military or paramilitary organization might be easier to infiltrate or penetrate.

### Sniper Code by M.Kryzhanovsky

1. Don't watch the target instead of your aiming point.
2. Don't jerk at the moment your weapon fires .
3. Apply wind as needed.
4. Never fire from the edge of a wood line – you should fire from a position inside the wood line (in the shade of shadows).
5. Do not cause overhead movement of trees, bushes or tall grasses by rubbing against them, move very slowly.
6. Do not use trails, roads or footpaths, avoid built-up and populated areas and areas of heavy enemy guerrilla activity.
7. Your position :

maximum fields of fire and observation of the target area, concealment from enemy observation, covered routes into and out of the position, located no closer than 300 meters from the target area, a natural or man-made obstacle between the position and the target area.

Place yourself under logs in a deadfall area, tunnels bored from one side of a knoll to the other, swamps, deep shadows, inside rubble piles.

Avoid positions close to isolated objects, at bends or ends of roads, trails or streams, in populated areas, unless it's required.

8. Do not fire from one position.
9. Don't stay in places with heavy traffic!
10. Key target - enemy sniper.
11. Train yourself to shoot while you stand, sit, lie, walk, run, jump, fall down; shoot at voices, shoot in a dark room, different weather and distance, day and night; shoot one object and a group; use one gun, two guns, gun and submachine gun (some doctrines train a sniper to breathe deeply before shooting, then hold their lungs empty while he lines up and

takes his shot; other go further, teaching a sniper to shoot between heartbeats to minimize barrel motion)

12. At distances over 300 m attempt body shots, aiming at the chest; at lesser distances attempt head shots (the most effective range is 300 to 600 meters).

13. Shoot from flanks and rear.

14. Never approach the body until you shoot it several times . Careful: the object could be wearing a bulletproof vest

15. It's important to get to the place, but it's more important to get out alive

16. Remember
- in hot weather bullets travel higher, in cold - lower
- a silencer reduces the maximum effective range of the weapon.

17. For moving targets, the point of aim is in front of the target ( it's called "Leading" the target, where the amount of lead depends on the speed and angle of the target's movement. For this technique, holding over is the preferred method.

18. The key to sniping is consistency.

19. Practical tips.

Angered and enraged man hears very badly - you have to develop "combat indifference" and complete immunity to stressful situations.

You can hear better when the area is illuminated. Green color also makes hearing more acute - it's the peculiarity of the nervous system. You massage the ears.

Sugar significantly increases the efficiency of night vision and hearing. You can chew a pinch of tea with a pinch of sugar and it reduces the time to adapt to the darkness from 30-40 to 5-7 minutes. The same effect is achieved by wiping his forehead, temples and neck with cold water. Night vision is exacerbated in the sitting position though nobody knows why.

Focused attention enhances night vision and hearing by 1.5-2 times, as well as light tapping massage with fingertips on closed eyelids

If you have normal vision, you must clearly see objects the size of 1mm at a distance of 4 metres.

Sniper needs a special diet, namely, vitamin A (carrots, blueberries).

Reading 1 hour on your back and watching TV more than 2 hours worsen your eyesight for 3 days.

To get rid of fatigue close your eyes from time to time for 5-10 seconds.

At night may need to look at the map - use only the red light. don't look at the bright lights as it might reduce your ability to see clearly for half an hour.

Not smoking ! Nicotine "squeezes" blood vessels, reduces visual acuity and increases the pulse.

The best sport for a sniper is swimming which develops the necessary muscle groups quickly.

**U.S. President's Security**

The top priority in protecting the President's life must be organized and complete intelligence. Any information from any person from any country concerning the President's personal security has to be immediately analyzed, and immediate action has to be performed. This is the first priority for intelligence and counter-intelligence agencies and police as well as the Secret Service. If the system is organized properly, nobody could even get in a position to try to shoot. Of course, the safest thing is to restrict the President's routes to government buildings only; but he has to travel and he has to travel abroad, too. Still, the President should leave his Office only when he really has to.

Since the President has to be let out from time to time, the newer technique is to restrict where the onlookers may congregate, especially those who wish to take the opportunity to express dismay with Presidential policies. Thus we now see the evolution of "free speech corners" so that demonstrators are confined to specific areas far from the actual event where the President is appearing or the route he is transiting.

### Presidential appearances

1. The Secret Service must have a top-secret plan of all visits, because the advance group has to come to the place at least a week ahead and cooperate with the field FBI offices and police (foreign special services if it's a visit abroad) paying attention to extremist groups and organizations. Officers and technicians search the place, looking for possible explosives, radioactive, biological and chemical dangerous or poisonous stuff and weapons; they check the walls, floors and ceilings; check air and water in the area; install weapons and explosives detectors and stay at the place 24/7, using night vision devices, too. (Dogs are good helpers if there is any question of explosives.) You have to check nearby houses as well (there could be people with mental health problems or dangerous criminals. Remember, the President must not appear in open areas close to apartment buildings. And the President has to be able to reach the National Security Command Center at any time.

2. If the President has to make a speech in open area there should be at least 3 security circles around him:

- up to 50 ft (personal bodyguards, weapons and explosives technicians)
- up to 200 ft (fast reaction anti-terror group)

- up to 1000 ft (support groups, snipers, police)

The security system includes both "open" and undercover groups (obvious security and people who play the crowd or service — drivers, waiters, cleaners — terrorists don't pay attention to them, as a rule). Each group follows its instructions strictly and avoids mess (personal bodyguards are in charge of immediate protection, anti-terror group has to fight and chase terrorists, etc.). Extra people always mean extra danger, so the most secure situation is when extra people have no access to the President at all and can't get into any of three circles. The guest list has to be triple checked to exclude anybody with criminal records who could compromise the leader. Reporters are there too and you have to tell them exactly where to wait (they have to be checked and kept separate after that), where to stand and what pictures (poses) to take; the President can't look stupid or funny. Inside the building watch when people applaud, stand up and sit down — terrorists prefer these situations to shoot or blow explosives.

When President moves through or along the crowd, "cut" it into pieces, guard him in circles, watch people who are carrying any objects (no flowers!) — they must not approach him; watch people with hands in their pockets, those who try to touch him, shake his hand, pass any object (gift, picture, photo). They must not be allowed to do that. If anybody behaves in a suspicious way, hold him tight (so he can't take out a gun) and "screw" him out of the crowd. In case of any attempt push the President to the ground, cover him and shoot immediately. Then leave the place as soon as possible and bring him to the hospital for a check up (even if he's OK).

**Frequent security mistakes**

The worst one - Secret Service and other agencies get inadequate intelligence information on a possible attempt or overlook important information, including anonymous letters and mail from psychos. (They must have information, even if it's "inside" the White House conspiracy. Agents have to memorize pictures of all the most dangerous persons who are wanted in the United States and people who were involved in attempted attacks on top politicians worldwide.)

The next two — extraneous people are allowed access to the President or extraneous people stay in the area close enough to shoot the President. In 1997, a France Press reporter took a picture of the Clintons dancing during their vacation on the Virgin Islands — they were dressed for the Caribbean and were happy in their privacy. Luckily, it was just a reporter, but what if it had been a sniper? What was the Secret Service doing? Then the picture was published worldwide and Hillary Clinton was furious - she didn't look attractive at all.

The last two major errors occur when (1) you can't identify the potential terrorists in the crowd and (2) you react too slow or waste time evacuating the President.

### Bonus. I saved Hillary Clinton

On August 9, 2006 at 8 A.M. I saw strange green flyers inside the Lefrak City, Queens buildings saying that: "State Senator John Sabini invites you to meet U.S. Senator Hillary Clinton on the issues. Lefrak City (by the pool). Wednesday, August 9, 2 P.M. Call Sabini for Senate at 718-651-8190 if you have any questions".

Unbelievable.

Do you know what's Lefrak City ? It's 20 old brick 18-floor projects for poor African-Americans, Latinos, and Russians. The most dangerous area in Queens and the New York State, stuffed with street gangs, crack cocaine, heroine, prostitutes and illegal guns. Three years ago 100 NYPD officers stormed the ghetto and arrested 13 most ruthless gangsters who terrorized people for years (another 10 are still wanted), confiscated guns, ammunition, drugs and $2.5 million in cash. On August 1, 2006 NYS Senator John Sabini delivered a speech at Lefrak City community meeting at St. Paul's Church demanding new, severe state and federal laws to control illegal weapons. And now, the same Sabini invites everybody to meet in person a former First Lady, the U.S. Senator Hillary Clinton at some open playground. What's that ? A sweet candy for terrorists? A regular stupidity?

I saw flyers at 8 A.M. , and in two minutes I was already walking to the place – just to make sure Mrs. Clinton, who saved my family, will meet the voters guarded by the "best of the best" – the U.S. Secret Service.

I was sure they already watch the area for the last 24 hours.

I was sure the access to the area is restricted.

I was sure that one week before the event local police instructed the secret sources to stay at alert and report any suspicious activity and people who had or tried to purchase illegal guns.

I was sure bad guys and aggressive psychos were isolated temporarily or kept under control at least.

I was sure technicians checked the air, soil and water (in the open pool) for radioactivity and toxic substances, looked for explosives and brought a specially trained dog.

I was sure there was no access to a single roof and they've

installed a metal detector to check VIP and other guests.
I was sure they had a double checked guest list. Kill me,
I was sure the Secret Service would never let any bad guy
approach Hillary Clinton. I was wrong.

At 8.30 A.M., six hours before the meeting, I came there to
check the place and estimate the threats.
Nothing and nobody around.
The place was a heaven for terrorists:
- a circle of six 18-floor-1500-window buildings (such
meetings in the open areas close to residential buildings are
strictly f o r b i d d e n )
- a playground
- an open stage under a small roof (no walls)
- barbeque place
- a pool

And six hours to get ready for assassination:
- observe the place and then plan assassination
- install a mine under a stage
- try a silenced sniper rifle out of any window or from the
roof and make necessary corrections
- bring and place the whole army of terrorists all over the
place

I've checked one of the building - free access to the roof.
Perfect conditions for a sniper.

At 11 A.M. two girls, three assistants and free "Pepsi"
appeared out of nowhere. 2 cops – in and out. No restriction.
Not even a "Don't cross" tape.
At 1 P.M. about 500 people came to the playground –

retired old men and women, homeless alcoholics,drug addicts, kids,teens and reporters.

At 2.30 P.M. people surrounded the playground and screamed like crazy when Hillary Clinton finally appeared among them and tried to make her way through the crowd. Anybody could touch or hit her - 2 cops and 2 Secret Service agents just smiled happily. Then she got to the stage encircled by a wild , absolutely uncontrolled crowd. One agent was standing behind her, another one – at the stairs. No security. I had to move close to the stage – the situation was unpredictable and I could help to protect Mrs. Clinton with my 10 years of KGB experience and 2 years of "The Nabat" anti-terror group.

She made a 15 minutes speech and then I've witnessed a total chaos – still on the stage, she tried to shake hands and people went wild; somebody gave her flowers (absolutely unacceptable thing), somebody asked her to hold a baby to make pictures; people screamed and pushed each other. I had to ask people to move back and some did. I was at the stage, right at the middle and people couldn't reach Hillary Clinton easily, some women tried to push me - I was laughing and playing a nice guy, but didn't leave my spot.

Agents paid no attention – they were slowly chewing gums, obviously proud of their James Bond style sunglasses. Poor Sabini asked people to move away – nobody cared. Only when some young girls jumped up on the stage, police officer reluctantly restricted the place with a yellow tape – the Secret Service guy looked at him insurprise. Then Hillary turned over to talk to somebody on the stage , and the agent turned his back to the crowd, too – I couldn't believe it.

At 3.30 she left the playground and had to move through the huge crowd again. I was next to her pretending I'm making video. She was lucky - God loves her. I love her too.

.

## DRUGS

We are the world's larger consumer of cocaine . I think that's a straight *national security threat.* Not just a threat – a complete, total catastrophe. Drugs sale money and terrorism always walk together. International picture looks really bad. We have no other choice but to start Global War on Drugs, if we want to protect and save America. Look what international drug dealers are doing – it's a global terror, isn't it ?

*Afghanistan.* World's largest producer of opium; 80-90% of the heroin consumed in Europe comes from Afghan opium; vulnerable to narcotics money laundering through informal financial networks.

*Albania.* Increasingly active transshipment point for Southwest Asian opiates, hashish, and cannabis transiting the Balkan route and - to a lesser extent - cocaine from South America destined for Western Europe .

*Angola.* A transshipment point for cocaine destined for Western Europe and other African states, particularly South Africa.

*Anguilla* . A transshipment point for South American narcotics destined for the US and Europe. *Antigua and Barbuda.* It is considered a minor transshipment point for narcotics bound for the US and Europe; more significant as an offshore financial center.

*Argentina.* A transshipment country for cocaine headed for Europe; some money-laundering activity, especially in the Tri-Border Area .

*Aruba* . A transit point for US- and Europe-bound narcotics with some accompanying money-laundering activity .

*Australia.* Tasmania is one of the world's major suppliers

of illicit opiate products . *Austria.* A transshipment point for Southwest Asian heroin and South American cocaine destined for Western Europe.

*Azerbaijan.* Limited illicit cultivation of cannabis and opium poppy, mostly for CIS consumption; small government eradication program; transit point for Southwest Asian opiates bound for Russia and to a lesser extent the rest of Europe.

*Bahamas* . A transshipment point for cocaine and marijuana bound for US and Europe; offshore financial center.

*Bangladesh* . A transit country for illegal drugs produced in neighboring countries.

*Barbados* . One of many Caribbean transshipment points for narcotics bound for Europe and the US; offshore financial center.

*Belgium.* Fast growing producer of synthetic drugs and cannabis; transit point for US-bound ecstasy; source of precursor chemicals for South American cocaine processors; transshipment point for cocaine, heroin, hashish, and marijuana entering Western Europe .

*Belize.* Transshipment point for cocaine; money-laundering activity related to narcotics trafficking and offshore sector.

*Benin.* Transshipment point used by Nigerian traffickers for narcotics destined for Western Europe; vulnerable to money laundering due to poorly enforced financial regulations.

*Bolivia.* World's third-largest cultivator of coca (after Colombia and Peru) with an estimated 26,500 hectares under cultivation in August 2005, an 8% increase from 2004; transit country for Peruvian and Colombian cocaine destined for Brazil, Argentina, Chile, Paraguay, and Europe; money-laundering activity related to narcotics trade, especially along t he borders with Brazil and Paraguay.

*Bosnia and Herzegovina* .Increasingly a transit point for

heroin being trafficked to Western Europe; remains highly vulnerable to money-laundering activity given a primarily cash-based and unregulated economy, weak law enforcement, and instances of corruption .

*Brazil.* Illicit producer of cannabis; important transshipment country for Bolivian, Colombian, and Peruvian cocaine headed for Europe; also used by traffickers as a way station for narcotics air transshipments between Peru and Colombia; upsurge in drug-related violence and weapons smuggling; important market for Colombian, Bolivian, and Peruvian cocaine; illicit narcotics proceeds earned in Brazil are often laundered through the financial system; significant illicit financial activity in the Tri-Border Area .

*British Virgin Islands.* A transshipment point for South American narcotics destined for the US and Europe; large offshore financial center makes it vulnerable to money laundering.

*Bulgaria.* Major European transshipment point for Southwest Asian heroin and, to a lesser degree, South American cocaine for the European market; limited producer of precursor chemicals; some money laundering of drug-related proceeds through financial institutions. *Burma* . It remains world's second largest producer of illicit opium; major source of methamphetamine and heroin for regional consumption .

*Canada.* Illicit producer of cannabis for the domestic drug market and export to US; increasing ecstasy production, some of which is destined for the US; vulnerable to narcotics money laundering because of its mature financial services sector.

*Cape Verde.* A transshipment point for Latin American cocaine destined for Western Europe; the lack of a well-developed financial system limits the country's utility as a money-laundering center.

*Cayman Islands* . Offshore financial center; vulnerable to drug transshipment to the US and Europe.

*Chile.* Important transshipment country for cocaine destined for Europe; economic prosperity and increasing trade have made Chile more attractive to traffickers seeking to launder drug profits, especially through the Iquique Free Trade Zone .

*China.* Major transshipment point for heroin produced in the Golden Triangle region of Southeast Asia; growing domestic drug abuse problem; source country for chemical precursors, despite new regulations on its large chemical industry .

*Colombia.* Illicit producer of coca, opium poppy, and cannabis; world's leading coca cultivator with 144,000 hectares in coca cultivation in 2005, a 26% increase over 2004, producing a potential of 545 t of pure cocaine; the world's largest producer of coca derivatives; supplies cocaine to most of the US market and the great majority of other international drug market; a significant portion of non-US narcotics proceeds are either laundered or invested in Colombia through the black market peso exchange; important supplier of heroin to the US market.

*Congo.* One of Africa's biggest producers of cannabis, but mostly for domestic consumption; while rampant corruption and inadequate supervision leaves the banking system vulnerable to money laundering, the lack of a well-developed financial system limits the country's utility as a money-laundering center .

*Costa Rica.* A transshipment country for cocaine and heroin from South America . *Croatia.* A transit point along the Balkan route for Southwest Asian heroin to Western Europe; has been used as a transit point for maritime shipments of

South American cocaine bound for Western Europe .

*Cuba*. Territorial waters and air space serve as transshipment zone for US- and European-bound drugs; established the death penalty for certain drug-related crimes in 1999.

*Cyprus.* A minor transit point for heroin and hashish via air routes and container traffic to Europe, especially from Lebanon and Turkey; some cocaine transits as well; despite a strengthening of anti-money-laundering legislation, remains vulnerable to money laundering; reporting of suspicious transactions in offshore sector remains weak.

*Czech Republic .* A transshipment point for Southwest Asian heroin and minor transit point for Latin American cocaine to Western Europe; producer of synthetic drugs for local and regional markets; susceptible to money laundering related to drug trafficking, organized crime. *Dominican Republic.* A transshipment point for South American drugs destined for the US and Europe; has become a transshipment point for ecstasy from the Netherlands and Belgium destined for US and Canada; substantial money laundering activity; Colombian narcotics traffickers favor the Dominican Republic for illicit financial transactions .

*Ecuador.* Significant transit country for cocaine originating in Colombia and Peru, with over half of the US-bound cocaine passing through Ecuadorian Pacific waters; importer of precursor chemicals used in production of illicit narcotics; attractive location for cash-placement by drug traffickers laundering money because of dollarization and weak anti-money-laundering regime; increased activity on the northern frontier by trafficking groups and Colombian insurgents.

*Egypt.* A transit point for cannabis, heroin, and opium moving to Europe, Israel, and North Africa; transit stop for Nigerian drug couriers; concern as money laundering site due to lax enforcement of financial regulations.

*El Salvador.* A transshipment point for cocaine.

*Estonia.* A growing producer of synthetic drugs; increasingly important transshipment zone for cannabis, cocaine, opiates, and synthetic drugs since joining the European Union.

*Ethiopia.* A transit hub for heroin originating in Southwest and Southeast Asia and destined for Europe, as well as cocaine destined for markets in southern Africa.

*France: Metropolitan France:* transshipment point for South American cocaine, Southwest Asian heroin.

*French Guiana.* A minor transshipment point to Europe.

*Georgia.* A transshipment point for opiates via Central Asia to Western Europe and Russia. *Germany* . This country is a source of precursor chemicals for South American cocaine processors; transshipment point for and consumer of Southwest Asian heroin, Latin American cocaine, and European-produced synthetic drugs; major financial center .

*Ghana.* Illicit producer of cannabis for the international drug *trade; major transit hub for Southwest and Southeast Asian heroin and, to a lesser extent, South American* cocaine destined for Europe and the US; widespread crime and money laundering problem, but the lack of a well developed financial infrastructure limits the country's utility as a money laundering center . *Greece.* A gateway to Europe for traffickers smuggling cannabis and heroin from the Middle East and Southwest Asia to the West and precursor chemicals to the East; some South American cocaine transits or is consumed in Greece.

Guatemala . A major transit country for cocaine and heroin; proximity to Mexico makes Guatemala a major staging area for drugs (particularly for cocaine).

*Guinea-Bissau* . An increasingly important transit country for South American cocaine en route to Europe; enabling environment for trafficker operations thanks to pervasive corruption. *Guyana* . A transshipment point for narcotics from South America - primarily Venezuela - to Europe and the US; producer of cannabis; rising money laundering related to drug trafficking and human smuggling.

*Haiti* .Caribbean transshipment point for cocaine en route to the US and Europe; substantial bulk cash smuggling activity; Colombian narcotics traffickers favor Haiti for illicit financial transactions.

*Hong Kong.* Despite strenuous law enforcement efforts, faces difficult challenges in controlling transit of heroin and methamphetamine to regional and world markets; modern banking system provides conduit for money laundering.

*Hungary* . A transshipment point for Southwest Asian heroin and cannabis and for South American cocaine destined for Western Europe; limited producer of precursor chemicals, particularly for amphetamine and methamphetamine .

*India.* It's world's largest producer of licit opium for the pharmaceutical trade, but an undetermined quantity of opium is diverted to illicit international drug markets; transit point for illicit narcotics produced in neighboring countries; illicit producer of methaqualone; illicit ketamine and precursor production.

*Indonesia* .Producer of methamphetamine and ecstasy.

*Iran* . Despite substantial interdiction efforts, Iran remains a key transshipment point for Southwest Asian heroin to Europe; highest percentage of the population in the world using opiates; lacks anti-money-laundering laws.

*Ireland* . A transshipment point for and consumer of hashish from North Africa to the UK and Netherlands and of European-produced synthetic drugs; increasing consumption of South American cocaine; minor transshipment point for heroin and cocaine destined for Western Europe; despite recent legislation, narcotics-related money laundering - using bureaux de change, trusts, and shell companies involving the offshore financial community - remains a . *Israel* . It's increasingly concerned about ecstasy, cocaine, and heroin abuse; drugs arrive in country from Lebanon and, increasingly, from Jordan; money-laundering center.

*Italy.* An important gateway for and consumer of Latin American cocaine and Southwest Asian heroin entering the European market.

*Jamaica* . A transshipment point for cocaine from South America to North America and Europe; substantial money-laundering activity; Colombian narcotics traffickers favor Jamaica for illicit financial transactions .

*Kazakhstan.* A significant illicit cultivation of cannabis for CIS markets, as well as limited cultivation of opium poppy; transit point for Southwest Asian narcotics bound for Russia and the rest of Europe .

*Kenya.* A transit country for South Asian heroin destined for Europe and North America; significant potential for money-laundering activity given the country's status as a regional financial center; massive corruption.

*North Korea.* For years, from the 1970s into the 2000s, citizens of the Democratic People's Republic of (North) Korea (DPRK), many of them diplomatic employees of the government, were apprehended abroad while trafficking in narcotics, including two in Turkey in December 2004; police investigations in Taiwan and Japan in recent years have linked North Korea to large illicit shipments of heroin and methamphetamine, including an attempt by the North Korean merchant ship Pong Su to deliver 150 kg of heroin to Australia in April 2003 .

*Kyrgyzstan.* A transit point for Southwest Asian narcotics bound for Russia and the rest of Europe.

*Latvia .*A transshipment and destination point for cocaine, synthetic drugs, opiates, and cannabis from Southwest Asia, Western Europe, Latin America, and neighboring Balkan countries .

*Liberia.* A transshipment point for Southeast and Southwest Asian heroin and South American cocaine for the European and US markets.

*Lithuania.* A transshipment and destination point for cannabis, cocaine, ecstasy, and opiates from Southwest Asia, Latin America, Western Europe, and neighboring Baltic countries; growing production of high-quality amphetamines.

*Macau.* A transshipment point for drugs going into mainland China .

*Macedonia.* A major transshipment point for Southwest Asian heroin and hashish; minor transit point for South American cocaine.

*Madagascar.* A transshipment point for heroin .

*Malta.* A minor transshipment point for hashish from North Africa to Western Europe. *Martinique.* A transshipment point for cocaine and marijuana bound for the US and Europe.

*Mauritius.* A consumer and transshipment point for heroin from South Asia.

*Mexico.* A major drug-producing country; continues as the primary transshipment country for US-bound cocaine from South America, with an estimated 90% of annual cocaine movements towards the US stopping in Mexico; major drug syndicates control majority of drug trafficking throughout the country; producer and distributor of ecstasy; significant money-laundering center; major supplier of heroin and largest foreign supplier of marijuana and methamphetamine to the

US market.

*Moldova* . A limited cultivation of opium poppy and cannabis, mostly for CIS consumption; transshipment point for illicit drugs from Southwest Asia via Central Asia to Russia, Western Europe, and possibly the US .

*Morocco.* One of the world's largest producers of illicit hashish; shipments of hashish mostly directed to Western Europe; transit point for cocaine from South America destined for Western Europe.

*Mozambique.* Southern African transit point for South Asian hashish and heroin, and South American cocaine probably destined for the European and South African markets.

*Nepal.* Illicit producer of cannabis and hashish for the domestic and international drug markets; transit point for opiates from Southeast Asia to the West.

*Netherlands.* A major European producer of synthetic drugs, including ecstasy, and cannabis cultivator; important gateway for cocaine, heroin, and hashish entering Europe; major source of US-bound ecstasy; large financial sector vulnerable to money laundering .

*Netherlands Antilles* .A transshipment point .for South American drugs bound for the US and Europe; money-laundering center.

*Nicaragua.* A transshipment point for cocaine destined for the US and transshipment point for arms-for-drugs dealing.

*Nigeria.* A transit point for heroin and cocaine intended for European, East Asian, and North American markets .

*Pakistan.* A key transit point for Afghan drugs, including heroin, opium, morphine, and hashish, bound for Western markets, the Gulf States, and Africa.

*Panama.* A major cocaine transshipment point and primary money-laundering center for narcotics revenue; money-laundering activity is especially heavy in the Colon Free Zone.

*Paraguay.* A major illicit producer of cannabis, most or all of which is consumed in Brazil, Argentina, and Chile.

*Peru.* Until 1996 the world's largest coca leaf producer, Peru is now the world's second largest producer of coca leaf, though it lags far behind Colombia; much of the cocaine base is shipped to neighboring Colombia for processing into cocaine, while finished cocaine is shipped out from Pacific ports to the international drug market; increasing amounts of base and finished cocaine, however, are being moved to Brazil and Bolivia for use in the Southern Cone or transshipped to Europe and Africa.

*Poland.* A minor transshipment point for Southwest Asian heroin and Latin American cocaine to Western Europe.

*Portugal.* Seizing record amounts of Latin American cocaine destined for Europe; a European gateway for Southwest Asian heroin; transshipment point for hashish from North Africa to Europe; consumer of Southwest Asian heroin .

*Romania.* A major transshipment point for Southwest Asian heroin transiting the Balkan route and small amounts of Latin American cocaine bound for Western Europe.

*Russia.* Limited cultivation of illicit cannabis and opium poppy and producer of methamphetamine, mostly for domestic consumption; used as transshipment point for Asian opiates, cannabis, and Latin American cocaine bound for growing domestic markets, to a lesser extent Western and Central Europe, and occasionally to the US; major source of heroin precursor chemicals; major consumer of opiates.

*Saint Kitts and Nevis.* A transshipment point for South American drugs destined for the US and Europe; some money-laundering activity.

*Saint Lucia.* A transit point for South American drugs

destined for the US and Europe.

*Saint Martin.* A transshipment point for Southwest Asian heroin moving to Western Europe on the Balkan route; economy vulnerable to money laundering.

*Saint Vincent and Grenadine.* A transshipment point for South American drugs destined for the US and Europe.

*Senegal.* A transshipment point for Southwest and Southeast Asian heroin and South American cocaine moving to Europe and North America. *Serbia.* A transshipment point for Southwest Asian heroin moving to Western Europe on the Balkan route.

*Serbia and Montenegro.* A transshipment point for Southwest Asian heroin moving to Western Europe on the Balkan route.

*Slovakia.* A transshipment point for Southwest Asian heroin bound for Western Europe; producer of synthetic drugs for regional market.

*Slovenia.* A minor transit point for cocaine and Southwest Asian heroin bound for Western Europe, and for precursor chemicals.

*South Africa.* A transshipment center for heroin, hashish, and cocaine, as well as a major cultivator of marijuana in its own right; cocaine and heroin consumption on the rise; world's largest market for illicit methaqualone, usually imported illegally from India through various east African countries, but increasingly producing its own synthetic drugs for domestic consumption; attractive venue for money launderers given the increasing level of organized criminal and narcotics activity in the region and the size of the South African economy.

*Spine.* Despite rigorous law enforcement efforts, North African, Latin American, Galician, and other European traffickers take advantage of Spain's long coastline to land large shipments of cocaine and hashish for distribution to the European market; consumer for Latin American cocaine and North African hashish; destination and minor transshipment point for Southwest Asian heroin; money-laundering site for Colombian narcotics trafficking organizations and organized crime.

*Suriname* . A growing transshipment point for South American drugs destined for Europe via the Netherlands and Brazil; transshipment point for arms-for-drugs dealing.

*Switzerland.* A transit country for and consumer of South American cocaine, Southwest Asian heroin, and Western European synthetics. *Syria.* A transit point for opiates, hashish, and cocaine bound for regional and Western markets; weak anti-money-laundering controls and bank privatization may leave it vulnerable to money laundering .

*Taiwan.* A regional transit point for heroin, methamphetamine, and precursor chemicals .

*Tajikistan* . A major transit country for Afghan narcotics bound for Russian and, to a lesser extent, Western European markets; Tajikistan seizes roughly 80% of all drugs captured in Central Asia and stands third worldwide in seizures of opiates (heroin and raw opium); significant consumer of opiates .

*Tanzania* .A growing role in transshipment of Southwest and Southeast Asian heroin and South American cocaine destined for South African, European, and US markets and of South Asian methaqualone bound for southern Africa .

Thailand. A minor producer of opium, heroin, and marijuana; transit point for illicit heroin en route to the international drug market from Burma and Laos .

*Timor-Leste Togo.* A transit hub for Nigerian heroin and cocaine traffickers.

*Trinidad and Tobago.* A transshipment point for South

American drugs destined for the US and Europe; producer of cannabis.

*Turkey.* A key transit route for Southwest Asian heroin to Western Europe and, to a lesser extent, the US - via air, land, and sea routes; major Turkish and other international trafficking organizations operate out of Istanbul; laboratories to convert imported morphine base into heroin exist in remote regions of Turkey and near Istanbul .

*Turkmenistan.* A transit country for Afghan narcotics bound for Russian and Western European markets; transit point for heroin precursor chemicals bound for Afghanistan . Turks and Caicos Islands .A transshipment point for South American narcotics destined for the US and Europe. *Ukraine.* Limited cultivation of cannabis and opium poppy, mostly for CIS consumption; some synthetic drug production for export to the West; limited government eradication program; used as transshipment point for opiates and other illicit drugs from Africa, Latin America, and Turkey to Europe and Russia.

*United Arab Emirates.* The UAE is a drug transshipment point for traffickers given its proximity to Southwest Asian drug-producing countries; the UAE's position as a major financial center makes it vulnerable to money laundering; anti-money-laundering controls improving, but informal banking remains unregulated .

*United Kingdom.* Producer of limited amounts of synthetic drugs and synthetic precursor chemicals; major consumer of Southwest Asian heroin, Latin American cocaine, and synthetic drugs; money-laundering center.

*United States.* The world's largest consumer of cocaine, shipped from Colombia through Mexico and the Caribbean; consumer of ecstasy and of Mexican heroin, marijuana and methamphetamine; minor consumer of high-quality Southeast

Asian heroin; illicit producer of cannabis, marijuana, depressants, stimulants, hallucinogens, and methamphetamine; money-laundering center.

*Uzbekistan.* A transit country for Afghan narcotics bound for Russian and, to a lesser extent, Western European markets; limited illicit cultivation of cannabis and small amounts of opium poppy for domestic consumption; poppy cultivation almost wiped out by government crop eradication program; transit point for heroin precursor chemicals bound for Afghanistan .

*Venezuela.* A small-scale illicit producer of opium and coca for the processing of opiates and coca derivatives; however, large quantities of cocaine, heroin, and marijuana transit the country from Colombia bound for US and Europe; significant narcotics-related money-laundering activity, especially along the border with Colombia and on Margarita Island .

*Vietnam.* A minor producer of opium poppy; probable minor transit point for Southeast Asian heroin.

*Zimbabwe .* A transit point for cannabis and South Asian heroin and methamphetamines en route to South Africa.

## Foreign Terrorist Organizations

Middle EastGaza and the West Bank
1.Abu Nidal Organization (ANO) (International, Palestinian)
2.Al-Aqsa Martyrs' Brigades (Palestinian)
3.HAMAS (Islamic Resistance Movement) (Palestinian)
4.Islamic Jihad Group (Palestinian)
5.Palestine Liberation Front (PLF) (Palestinian)
6.Popular Front for the Liberation of Palestine (PFLP) (Palestinian)
7.PFLP-General Command (PFLP-GC) (Palestinian)
Iraq
1.Ansar al-Islam (Iraqi Kurdistan)
2.Kata'ib Hezbollah (Iraq)
3.Kongra-Gel (formerly Kurdistan Workers' Party) (KGK, formerly PKK, KADEK, Kongra-Gel) (Turkey, Iraq, Iran, Syria)
4.Tanzim Qa'idat al-Jihad fi Bilad al-Rafidayn (QJBR) (al-Qaida in Iraq) (formerly Jama'at al-Tawhid wa'al-Jihad, JTJ, al-Zarqawi Network) (Iraq)
Lebanon
1.Asbat an-Ansar (Lebanon)
2.Hezbollah (Party of God) (Lebanon)
Israel
1.Kahane Chai (Kach) (Israel)
Iran
1.Mujahedin-e Khalq Organization (MEK) (Iran)
2.Jundallah (People's Resistance Movement of Iran, or PRMI) (Iran) [2]
Saudi Arabia
1.al-Qa'ida (Global)
2.al-Qa'ida in the Arabian Peninsula (AQAP)

3.al-Qa'ida in the Islamic Maghreb (formerly GSPC) (The Maghreb)
Asia
Japan
1.Aum Shinrikyo (China)
South East Asia
1.Jemaah Islamiya organization (JI)
Bangladesh
1.Harkat-ul-Jihad al-Islami (HUJI-B) (Bangladesh)
Sri Lanka
1.Liberation Tigers of Tamil Eelam (LTTE) (Sri Lanka)
Philippines
1.Abu Sayyaf Group (ASG) (Philippines)
2.Communist Party of the Philippines/New People's Army (CPP/NPA) (Philippines)
India
1.Indian Mujahideen (IM) (India)
Pakistan
1.Harakat ul-Mujahidin (HUM) (Pakistan)
2.Jaish-e-Mohammed (Army of Mohammed) (JEM) (Pakistan)
3.Lashkar-e Tayyiba (Army of the Righteous) (LET) (Muridke, Pakistan)
4.Lashkar i Jhangvi (Pakistan)
5.Tehrik-i-Taliban Pakistan (TTP) (Pakistan)
Uzbekistan
1.Islamic Movement of Uzbekistan (IMU) (Uzbekistan)
Africa1.Al-Shabaab (Somalia)
Algeria
1.Armed Islamic Group (GIA) (Algeria)
Egypt
1.Gama'a al-Islamiyya (Egypt)
2.Egyptian Islamic Jihad (Egypt)

Libya
1.Libyan Islamic Fighting Group (LIFG) (Libya)
Morocco
1.Moroccan Islamic Combatant Group (MICG) (Morocco)
EuropeUnited Kingdom and Republic of Ireland
1.Continuity Irish Republican Army (CIRA) (United Kingdom, Republic of Ireland)
2.Real Irish Republican Army (RIRA) (United Kingdom, Republic of Ireland)
3.Ulster Volunteer Force (UVF) (United Kingdom, Republic of Ireland)
4.Ulster Defence Association (UDA) (United Kingdom, Republic of Ireland)
Greece
1.Revolutionary Organization 17 November (Greece)
2.Revolutionary Struggle (Greece)
Turkey
1.Revolutionary People's Liberation Party/Front (DHKP/C) (Turkey)
Spain
1.Euskadi Ta Askatasuna (Basque Fatherland and Liberty) (ETA) (Spain, France)
South America
Colombia
1.National Liberation Army (ELN) (Colombia)
2.Revolutionary Armed Forces of Colombia (FARC) (Colombia)
3.United Self-Defense Forces of Colombia (AUC) (Colombia)
Peru
1.Shining Path (Sendero Luminoso, SL) (Peru)

**Law enforcement counter-terrorist organizations by**

**country**

Argentina: GEOF (Special Group of Federal Operations, Federal Police) Falcon Commando (Comando Halcon, State Buenos Aires Police)

Australia: State and Australian Federal Police, Police Tactical Groups, Australian Protective Service (APS), Tactical Assault Group (TAG East & TAG West), and Australian Security and Intelligence Organization (ASIO)

Austria: EKO Cobra+; Austrian Military Police+ (Kommando Militärstreife & Militärpolizei — Kdo MilStrf&MP)

Bangladesh: Rapid Action Battalion+; Police Swat; Bangladesh Para Commandos; Bangladesh Navy Special Warfare Diving and Salvage (BN SWADS)

Brazil: State/local Police SWAT teams: BOPE, COE, GATE, COT

Bosnia and Herzegovina: SIPA

Bulgaria:SOBT

Canada: JTF2

Chile: GOPE (Police Special Operations Group, Chilean Carabineros) ERTA (Tactic Reaction Team, PDI Chilean Civil Police)

China: Snow Leopard Commando Unit+, Beijing SWAT, Special Police Unit and Immediate Action Unit+

Croatia Luèko Anti-Terrorist Unit, RH Alfa

Czech: URNA National Police Rapid Response Unit or Útvar rychlého nasazení

Denmark: Politiets Aktionsstyrke

Dominican Republic: Anti-terrorism Special Command — Comando Especial Contra Terrorismo

Egypt: Unit 777

Estonia: K-Commando

Finland Karhu-ryhmä, Utti Jaeger Regiment, Guard Jaeger Regiment

France: Police units GIPN, RAID and Gendarmerie GIGN+

Germany: Police SEK / MEK, USK (Bavarian State Police), ZUZ and Bundespolizei GSG 9+

Greece: Anti-Terror Division, Greek Police and Special Anti-Terrorist Unit.

Hong Kong: Police Force Special Duties Unit, Airport Security Unit and Counter Terrorism Response Unit.

Hungary: Commando Neutron I-II.

Iceland: Víkingasveitin

India: NSG, Force One, State and Metropolitan Police Commandos

Indonesia: Detachment 88

Iran: NAJA Iranian Police, NOPO Team Anti-terror special force

Iraq: Iraqi Hillah Swat

Ireland: Emergency Response Unit (Garda), Irish Army Ranger Wing

Israel: YAMAM – elite Israeli Police anti-terror unit (counter-terror, foiling terrorism, hostages rescue etc.), "Mistaarvim" – IDF and Border Guard undercover units for foiling terrorism

Italy: NOCS, GIS

Japan: Special Assault Team, Special Security Team

Korea, South: 707th Special Mission Unit+

Latvia: OMEGA police unit

Lithuania: ARAS (Force) Lithuanian Police force of antiterrorism operations

Malaysia: Pasukan Gerakan Khas, UNGERIN, Rapid Actions Troops, STAR APMM

Netherlands:DSI+ (Dutch: Dienst Speciale Interventies, Special Interventions Service) and police special arrest

teams Royal Marechaussee(Dutch: Brigade Speciale Beveiligingsopdrachten, Special Security Task Brigade)Dutch marines BBE
New Zealand: Special Tactics Group, NZSAS Tactical Assault Group (TAG)
Norway: Beredskapstroppen, FSK+
Poland: GROM, SPAP
Portugal: GOE and COE
Pakistan: Special Service Group, Pakistan Army Rangers, and Elite Police Commandos
Philippines: PNP-Special Action Force, Philippine Navy-Naval Special Warfare Group, Coast Guard-Special Operations Group and police SWAT teams
Romania: Brigada Antiteroristã, (counter-terrorist brigade)
Russia: Spetsgruppa A, Vympel
Serbia: SAJ, PTJ
Sri Lanka: Special Task Force
Spain: GEO and UEI
Sweden: National Task Force (Nationella Insatsstyrkan) and Särskilda Skyddsgruppen (Special Protection Group)
Taiwan: Thunder Squad
Turkey: Özel tim-Özel Harekat Timi (Special Team) and Maroon Berets
Tunisia: BAT and USGN
UK: Counter Terrorism Command
Uruguay: GEO (Uruguayan Police) and Escorpión Commando Group (Uruguayan Army)
U.S.: FBI Hostage Rescue Team, Federal Air Marshal Service, Immigration and Customs Enforcement, BORTAC, state/local Police SWAT teams

# ESPIONAGE GLOSSARY

agent - a person, usually a foreign national, who has been recruited by a staff case officer from an intelligence service to perform clandestine missions

agent-in-place - an agent serving as a penetration into an intelligence target who has been recruited or has volunteered to stay in place

ambush - The surprise capture and arrest of a case officer and/or his agent in an act of espionage by an opposing counterintelligence or security service

asset - a clandestine source or method, usually an agent

bailout point - the point, during a vehicular run under surveillance, at which the action officer riding as a passenger is planning to bail out of the car in order to elude surveillance

bang and burn - demolition and sabotage operations

Barium meal test - revealing a secret to a suspected enemy (a "mole"), then monitor whether there is evidence of the fake information being utilized by the other side. For example, the double agent could be offered some tempting "bait" e.g. be told that important information was stored at a dead drop site. The fake dead drop site could then be periodically checked for signs of disturbance. If the site showed signs of being disturbed (in order to copy the microfilm stored there) then this would confirm that the suspected enemy really was an enemy e.g. a double agent.

black bag job - a surreptitious entry operation usually conducted by the FBI against a domestically located foreign intelligence target

black operations - clandestine or covert operations not attributable to the organization carrying them out

black room - any place or organization dedicated to code-breaking, its more exact meaning is a secret room in a post office, and, later and by extension, a telecommunications center used by state officials to conduct clandestine interception and surveillance of communications

bona fides - an operative's true identity, affiliation, or intentions bridge agent - an agent who acts as a courier or go-between from a case officer to an agent in a denied area

brief encounter - any brief physical contact between a case officer and an agent under threat of surveillance

brush pass - a brief encounter where something is passed between a case officer and an agent

bumper-lock - a harassing move in which vehicular surveillance follows the target officer so closely that the surveilling car's front bumper is almost locked to the rear bumper of the target car

burned - when a case officer or agent is compromised, or a surveillant has been made by a target, usually because they make eye contact

bust-out - a leak of electronic communications from a secure enclosure before they are encrypted by the code machine

cam-car - a vehicle equipped with a concealed camera used for clandestine casing and surveillance operations.

case officer - an operations officer serving as an official staffer of an intelligence service.

casuals - casual observers to a surveillance exercise; nonparticipants visible in the area.

chokepoint - a narrow passage-such as a bridge, tunnel, or Metro station-used as a surveillance or counter-surveillance tool for channeling the opposing force or monitoring their passage.

clandestine operation - an intelligence operation designed to remai

code - a system used to obscure a message by use of a cipher, mark, symbol, sound, innocuous verse, or piece of music

compartmenting: vertical; lateral; double - the various ways that information is held to only those who "have-a-need-to-know" in an organization. Vertical denies information up or down the chain of command, and lateral denies information from peer groups. Double is spoofing the original group who held the information into believing the operation has ended when it has simply moved to a new compartment.

compromised - when an operation, asset, or agent is uncovered and cannot remain secret.

concealment device - Any one of a variety of innocuous devices used to secretly store and transport materials relating to an operation.

control - in a surveillance exercise, the one directing the team remotely, usually by electronic communications

controller - often used interchangeably with handler, but usually means a hostile force is involved-that is, the agent has come under control of the opposition

cover stop - a stop made while under surveillance that provides an ostensibly innocent reason for a trip

covert action operation - an operation kept secret for only a finite period of time, or an operation whose

real source remains secret because the operation is attributed to another source

covert listening device (bug or a wire) - a combination of a miniature radio transmitter with amicrophone. The use of bugs, called bugging, is a common technique in surveillance, espionage and in police investigations. A bug does not have to be a device specifically designed for the purpose of eavesdropping. For instance, with the right equipment, it is possible to remotely activate the microphone of cellular phones, even when a call is not being made, to listen to conversations in the vicinity of the phone.

cryptonym - code name.

dangle operation - an operation in which an enticing intelligence target is dangled in front of an opposition service in hopes they will think him or her a bona fide recruit. The dangle is really a double agent.

cutout - mutually trusted intermediary, method or channel of communication, facilitating the exchange of information between agents. Cutouts usually only know the source and destination of the information to be transmitted, but are unaware of the identities of any other persons involved in the espionage process. Thus, a captured cutout cannot be used to identify members of an espionage cell.

dead drop – a method of espionage tradecraft used to pass

items between two individuals by using a secret location and thus does not require them to meet directly. Using a dead drop permits a case officer and his agent to exchange objects and information while maintaining operational security. The method stands in contrast to the live drop, so called because two persons meet to exchange items or information. The system involves using signals and locations which have been agreed upon in advance. These signals and locations must be common everyday things to which most people would not give a second glance. The signal may or may not be located close to the dead drop itself. The location of the dead drop could be a loose brick in a wall, a library book, a hole in a tree, or under a boulder etc. It should be something common and from which the items can be 'picked up' without the operatives being seen by a member of the public or the security forces who may be watching. The signaling devices can include a chalk mark on a wall, a piece of chewing-gum on a lamppost, a newspaper left on a park bench etc. Alternatively, the signal can be made from inside the agent's own home e.g. hanging a distinctively colored towel from a balcony, or placing a potted plant on a window sill where it is visible to anyone on the street. The dead drop is often used as a cut-out device. In this use the operatives who use the device to communicate or exchange materials or information do not know one another and should never see one another. While this type of device is useful in preventing the capture of an entire espionage network it is not foolproof. If the lower level operative is compromised he or she may reveal the location and signal for the use of the dead drop. Then the counter espionage agents simply use the signal to indicate that the dead drop is ready for pickup. They then keep the spot under continuous surveillance until it is picked up. They can then capture the operative who picked up the material from the dead drop. The dead drop spike is a concealment device similar to a microcache which has been used since the late 1960s to hide money, maps, documents, microfilm, and other items. The spike is waterproof and mildew-proof and can be shoved into the ground or placed in a shallow stream to be retrieved at a later time.

dead telephone - a signal or code passed with the telephone without speaking

defector - a person who has intelligence value who volunteers to work for another intelligence service. He may be requesting asylum or can remain in place

double agent - an agent who has come under the control of another intelligence service and is being used against his original handlers

eavesdropping - secret listening to the private conversation of others without their consent. It can be done over telephone lines (wiretapping), email, instant messaging, and other methods of communication considered private.

escort officer - the operations officer assigned to lead a defector along an exfiltration route

exfiltration operation - a clandestine rescue operation designed to get a defector, refugee, or operative and his or her family out of harm's way

(the) eye - the person on the surveillance team who has the target under visual observation at any given moment

foots (feet) - members of a surveillance team who are working on foot and riding as passengers in a surveillance car

front organization - any entity set up by and controlled by another organization, such as intelligence agencies, organized crime groups, banned organizations, religious or political groups, advocacy groups, or corporations. Front organizations can act for the parent group without the actions being attributed to the parent group. Front organizations that appear to be independent voluntary associations or charitable organizations are called front groups.

ghost surveillance - Extremely discreet and seemingly omnipresent surveillance, working mostly out of the view of the target.

illegal - a KGB operative infiltrated into a target country and operating without the protection of diplomatic immunity

impersonal communications - secret communication techniques used between a case officer and a human intelligence asset when no physical contact is possible or desired.

infiltration operation - the covert moving of an operative into a target area with the idea that his presence or true affiliation will go undetected for the appropriate amount of time.

in the black - surveillance-free for a time span greater than a few seconds

in the gap - surveillance-free for a few seconds but not as long as a minute

in the wind - when a target of surveillance has escaped and left for parts unknown

legend (cover) - the complete cover story developed for an operative

local agent - an agent recruited in a particular target area to do a local task

lockstep - when a surveillance team is following so close on foot they seem to be moving in lockstep with the target.

"L" pill - A lethal cyanide capsule issued to intelligence operatives who would prefer to take their own life rather than be caught and tortured

METKA - A KGB umbrella program that encompassed research on all their various tagging and marking substances, like spy dust.

microdot - a photographic reduction of a secret message so small it can be hidden in plain sight under the period at the end of this sentence

"mole" - a human penetration into an intelligence service or other highly sensitive organization. Quite often a mole is a defector who agrees to work in place.

Moscow rules - the ultimate tradecraft methods for use in the most hostile of the operational environments. During the Cold War, Moscow was considered the most difficult of operating environments.

one-time pad - sheets of paper or silk printed with random five-number group ciphers to be used to encode and decode enciphered messages

OP - an observation post manned by a static surveillant

operative - an intelligence officer or agent operating in the field

overhead platform - a technical platform, aboard an airplane or satellite, used for technical surveillance and reconnaissance.

OWVL - one-way voice link; shortwave radio link used to transmit prerecorded enciphered messages to an operative, who is usually working in place in a hostile area

passive probe - someone sent on an intelligence mission just to passively observe and record details about the target location or organization

pattern - the overt behavior and daily routine of an operative that makes his identity unique

PDB - The president's daily brief, the CIA briefing document delivered to the president of the United States first thing each day. It is always accompanied by a senior CIA officer.

personal meeting - a clandestine meeting between two operatives, always the most desirable but a more risky form of communication

PLASMA - a secret technique or device used to defeat a lock.

point - the member of the surveillance team who is following the target from the closest position, the point position

postal interception - retrieving another person's mail for the purpose of ensuring that the mail is not delivered to the recipient, or to spy on them

prober - an operative assigned to test border controls before an exfiltration is mounted. Usually a specialist in false documents.

profile - all the aspects of an operative's or a target's overt physical or behavioral persona

provocateur - an operative sent to incite a target group to action for purposes of entrapping or embarrassing them

provocative - a harassing act or procedure designed to flush out surveillance

put up a signal - to clandestinely signal another operative or secret source, as in putting up a signal like a chalk mark on a light pole

rabbit - the target in a surveillance operation

repro - making a false document.

rezident - a KGB chief of station in a foreign location, usually under diplomatic cover

rezidentura - a KGB station, usually located in their embassy in a foreign capital

roll-out - a surreptitious technique of rolling out the contents of a letter without opening it. It can be done with two knitting needles or a split chopstick

rolled up - when an operation goes bad and the agent is arrested

rolling car pickup - a clandestine car pickup executed so smoothly that the car hardly stops at all and seems to have kept moving forward.

safe house - an apartment, hotel room, or other similar site considered safe for use by operatives as a base of operations or for a personal meeting

silver bullet - the special disguise and deception tradecraft techniques developed under Moscow rules to help the CIA penetrate the KGB's security perimeter in Moscow

smoking-bolt operation - a covert snatch operation in which a special entry team breaks into an enemy installation and steals a high-security device, like a code machine, leaving nothing but the "smoking bolts."

spoofing - a ploy designed to deceive the observer into believing that an operation has gone bad when, in fact, it has been put into another compartment

spy dust - a chemical marking compound developed by the KGB to keep tabs on the activities of a target officer. Also called METKA. The compound is made of nitrophenyl pentadien (NPPD) and luminol.

stage management - managing the operational stage in a deception operation, so that all conditions and contingencies are considered: point of view of the hostile forces and the casual observers, physical and cultural environments, etc.

star-burst maneuver - a counter-surveillance ploy in which more than one target car or target officer is being followed and they suddenly go in different directions, forcing the surveillance team to make instant choices about whom to follow

steganography - the concealment of information within computer files. In digital steganography, electronic communications may include steganographic coding inside of a transport layer, such as a document file, image file, program or protocol. Media files are ideal for steganographic transmission because of their large size. As a simple example, a sender might start with an innocuous image file and adjust the color of every 100th pixel to correspond to a letter in the alphabet, a change so subtle that someone not specifically looking for it is unlikely to notice it.

stronghold - A foreign-based Soviet mission

SVR - The Russian foreign intelligence service that succeeded the KGB's First Chief Directorate.

swallow - a female operative who uses sex as a tool

timed drop - a dead drop that will be retrieved if it is not picked up by the intended recipient after a set time.

tosses (hand, vehicular) - tradecraft techniques for placing drops by tossing them while on the move

tradecraft - the methods developed by intelligence operatives to conduct their operations

tunnel sniffers - technical air sampler sensors designed to sniff for hostile substances or parties in a dark tunnel system

201 file - the file at CIA that contains all the personal information on a staff officer or an agent, including any training and operational details unique to the person

walk-in - a defector who declares his intentions by walking into an official installation, or otherwise making contact with an opposition government, and asking for political asylum or volunteering to work in place. Also known as a volunteer.

warming room - a location out of the weather where a surveillance team can go to keep warm and wait for the target

watcher team - a surveillance team usually assigned to a specific target

window dressing - ancillary materials that are included in a cover story or deception operation to help convince the opposition or casual observers that what they are observing is genuine

(The) Year of the Spy - The year 1985 was labeled "The Year of the Spy" by the media because of the number of espionage-related incidents that came to light that year. Unbeknownst to the media and the CIA at the time, several other significant spying ventures started during this same year and would not come to light until years later.

# Would you like to see your manuscript become a book?

If you are interested in becoming a PublishAmerica author, please submit your manuscript for possible publication to us at:

**acquisitions@publishamerica.com**

You may also mail in your manuscript to:

**PublishAmerica
PO Box 151
Frederick, MD 21705**

---

## We also offer free graphics for Children's Picture Books!

---

# www.publishamerica.com

CPSIA information can be obtained at www.ICGtesting.com
Printed in the USA
LVOW061717110512

281392LV00010B/22/P

9 781462 661602